CLOTHED IN CHRIST

A HOW-TO GUIDE

Edited by
ED GALLAGHER

Clothed in Christ: A How-to-Guide

Published by Heritage Christian University Press

Copyright © 2017, 2021 by Ed Gallagher

Manufactured in the United States of America

Cataloging-in-Publication Data

Clothed in Christ: A how-to-guide / edited by Ed Gallagher

p. cm.

Berean Study Series

Includes scripture index.

ISBN 978-1-7374751-8-7 (pbk.) 978-1-7374751-9-4 (ebook)

1. Christian life. I. Gallagher, Edmon, L. editor. II. Title. III. Series.

248.4—dc20

Library of Congress Control Number: 2021920139

Cover design by Brad McKinnon and Brittany Vander Maas.
All rights reserved. No part of this publication may be reproduced, distributed, stored in a retrieval system, or transmitted in any form or by any means without the prior written permission of the publisher, except in the case of brief quotations embodied in critical reviews and certain other noncommercial uses permitted by copyright law.

For information:
Heritage Christian University Press
3625 Helton Drive
PO Box HCU
Florence, AL 35630

www.hcu.edu

CONTENTS

Bible Abbreviations — v

1. BEING SPIRITUAL — 1
   Jim Collins

2. PRAYER — 8
   Bill Bagents

3. LIVING IN SCRIPTURE — 16
   Nathan Daily

4. BEING A SHEEP — 25
   Philip Goad

5. FRUIT OF THE SPIRIT — 34
   Ray Reynolds

6. WORSHIP — 40
   Matt Heupel

7. SPIRITUAL DISCIPLINE — 49
   Arvy Dupuy

8. EVANGELISM — 57
   Jeremy Barrier

9. MENTORING — 63
   Brad McKinnon

10. AUTHORITY — 71
    C. Wayne Kilpatrick

11. DYING TO SIN — 77
    Justin Guin

12. CHURCH INVOLVEMENT — 86
    Lucas Suddreth

13. HAVING REALISTIC EXPECTATIONS — 94
    Travis Harmon

Bibliography	101
Scripture Index	103
Credits	110
Contributors	112
Berean Study Series	116

BIBLE ABBREVIATIONS

Old Testament
Gen	Genesis
Exod	Exodus
Lev	Leviticus
Num	Numbers
Deut	Deuteronomy
Josh	Joshua
Judg	Judges
Ruth	Ruth
1–2 Sam	1–2 Samuel
1–2 Kgs	1–2 Kings
1–2 Chr	1–2 Chronicles
Ezra	Ezra
Neh	Nehemiah
Esth	Esther
Job	Job
Ps	Psalms
Prov	Proverbs

Eccl	Ecclesiastes
Song	Song of Solomon
Isa	Isaiah
Jer	Jeremiah
Lam	Lamentations
Ezek	Ezekiel
Dan	Daniel
Hos	Hosea
Joel	Joel
Amos	Amos
Obad	Obadiah
Jonah	Jonah
Mic	Micah
Nah	Nahum
Hab	Habakkuk
Zeph	Zephaniah
Hag	Haggai
Zech	Zechariah
Mal	Malachi

New Testament

Matt	Matthew
Mark	Mark
Luke	Luke
John	John
Acts	Acts
Rom	Romans
1–2 Cor	1–2 Corinthians
Gal	Galatians

Eph	Ephesians
Phil	Philippians
Col	Colossians
1–2 Thess	1–2 Thessalonians
1–2 Tim	1–2 Timothy
Titus	Titus
Phlm	Philemon
Heb	Hebrews
Jas	James
1–2 Pet	1–2 Peter
1–2–3 John	1–2–3 John
Jude	Jude
Rev	Revelation

1. BEING SPIRITUAL
JIM COLLINS

2 Peter 3:18

One Main Thing

Which is more important to you: to look spiritual or to be spiritual?

Introduction

Jesus came to the earth to bring forgiveness, redemption, salvation, and hope to lost people in the first century and for all of mankind throughout eternity (John 3:16). His ministry began among His own people, some of whom were spiritually empty and just going through the motions. Some of the Jewish spiritual leaders were worse off than others. Why? Because they placed a higher priority on looking spiritual than on being spiritual. Some of them had become arrogant, empty, and unacceptable to God. On one occasion, Jesus gave a scathing attack on their hypocrisy stating, "Woe to you, scribes and Pharisees, hypocrites! For you are like whitewashed tombs which indeed appear beautiful outwardly, but inside are full of dead men's bones and all uncleanness" (Matt 23:27). The people Jesus castigates presented themselves in public as pious and spiritual leaders, but it was fake, false and hypocritical. So, as Christians, how and where do we start in order to be genuinely spiritual?

I suggest we start with Jesus's teaching in the Sermon on the Mount. This was where He started with His own people in the first century and emphasized the need for these spiritual qualities. He gave them some serious, eye-opening teachings. He says we should begin our journey with a deeply rooted sense of humility and sorrow for our sin. We move on to have a hungering and thirsting for being righteous and spiritual (Matt 5:3–12). In v.8, He presents an important characteristic for growing spiritually as a person of God. Observe His teaching: "Blessed are the pure in heart [Gk.: "*kardia*"] for they shall see God" (Matt 5:8). The Jews understood the idea communicated by the word "heart" as a reference to the seat of the physical, spiritual, and mental life. It was the center of a person's whole inner life, with its thinking, feeling and decision-making. It is where God looks, in order to see the real person. In other words, it is more about our attitude of seeking God with

Being Spiritual

a deep-seated spiritual quest to truly know God and to be what God desires for us, rather than just going through the outward ceremonial motions.

The illustration of the man's approach to being spiritual vs. God's correct approach is described by Jesus in the parable of the Pharisee and the tax collector (Luke 18:9–14). In the text, the "Pharisee, stood and prayed thus within himself, 'God, I thank you that I am not like other men—extortioners, unjust, adulterers, or even as this tax collector.'" He also allows us to witness the humble non-judgmental approach made to Him by the tax collector. "And the tax collector, standing afar off, would not so much as raise his eyes to heaven, but beat his breast, saying, 'God, be merciful to me a sinner'" (Luke 18:13)! The important question for each of us is which of these approaches do we use when we go before God to the worship assembly and in the community where you live and work? Which attitude should we use in our approach to God in our everyday life, if we are genuinely seeking to be spiritual?

Once we determine the appropriate heart with which to approach God and make the journey for spiritual growth, we can begin. This is described by Jesus to a Jewish lawyer who was trying to trap Jesus when he asked, "What is the greatest law in the commandments?" Jesus explained the Great Commandment to the Pharisee: "You shall love the Lord your God with all you heart [*kardia*], with all your soul, and with all your mind" (Matt 22:37).

Application

How can I apply my spiritual heart to achieve the spiritual growth God wants me to have? First, I comprehend the importance of my love for God and desire to be a sincere person of God. After realizing God's great love, we are ready to begin the journey. If we love God with all our heart, soul and mind, we also desire to be humble enough to know we are not perfect. We make mistakes; We have sin in our lives. We know that we are not all that we can or should be for God. Therefore, we sincerely desire to be more spiritual.

Begin your spiritual journey with *an intense desire to grow* (Rom 12:1–2). Paul explains to Roman Christians that an intense desire to grow is about sincerely and deeply striving after the mind of Christ. Paul declares it is possible. It can happen when we make the choice to follow God's way rather than our own sinful way and/or Satan's. We make this choice, within ourselves, to become a willing sacrifice. It all starts in the mind, heart, and soul. We make a decision to study God's word more (2 Tim 2:15), to trust its direction (2 Tim 3:16–17), to read it, study it, and apply it to our life. We will pray deeply and often (Phil 4:6–7), while trying to live less for self and more for God and others; "Let nothing be done through selfish ambition or conceit,

Being Spiritual

but in lowliness of mind let each esteem others better than himself" (Phil 2:3). We will be conscious of how Satan works in our lives and will choose to not be overcome with the ways of the world and worldliness. We strive to have this deeper knowledge of self and make a conscientious effort from the heart to be spiritual.

Secondly, *seek to incorporate Christ-like attitudes and characteristics within*, (Phil 2:2; Gal 5:22–25; Rom 12:3–8). This will help in dealing with the world and people who may not always treat others fairly and respectfully. It has been said by some as "garbage in, garbage out." Therefore, rather than inputting un-Christ-like ideas, thoughts, and characteristics, we seek to input spiritual thoughts and godly characteristics. When you are incorporating spiritual qualities into your heart, mind, and center of life [*kardia*], you are laying a good foundation for being spiritual. You will strive to have a deep-rooted spiritual center and an expectation of responding in a godly, Christ-like way when faced with difficult and worldly situations. While others are being ugly, hateful, spiteful, and ungodly, you can respond respectfully, kindly, and caringly. When you respond in a Christ-like way, you will be demonstrating to the world that there is a better way of life.

Since you have the intense desire to grow and input the right thoughts and characteristics to be God's person, you have the solid, spiritual foundation. Once you have *implemented the use of Christ-like attitudes and actions*, people will see Christ truly living in you. You will strive to be without hypocrisy, abhor what is evil, and cling to what is good. You will seek to be kindly affectionate to others, serving the Lord. You can rejoice in hope, be more patient in tribulation, steadfast in prayer, help the needy, and be hospitable. You can even seek to bless those who are mean or mistreat you. Because you have the love of God in your heart, you will attempt to be more compassionate with those who are hurting, sick, sad, or lonely, and allow the Lord to respond to evil, while seeking to overcome evil with good (Rom 12:9–21; 1 Cor 13:1–8; Col 3:12–15).

Since you are striving daily to be like Christ, you can be more holy, loving, kind, humble, filled with meekness, full of tender mercy and patience, bearing with and forgiving others. Because you are striving to be a child of God, you recognize God's forgiveness for you and your sins, which requires you to forgive others. You can be spiritual, more thankful for how God has blessed you, and know that the peace of God rules in your heart and life (Phil 4:7, 9).

Discussion

1. Why is the heart of a person so important?
2. What is the significance of our heart when making a decision that pertains to our life and how we interact with others?

3. Explain the parallel of our lives in accordance to first century Jews.
4. What are some of the vital attitudes and characteristics that can help us be more spiritual?

2. PRAYER
BILL BAGENTS

Luke 11:1

One Main Thing

Like the unnamed disciple of Luke 11:1, we need to ask Jesus to teach us to pray because we cannot be like Jesus unless we pray like Jesus.

Introduction

Of all the ways to be clothed in Christ, none could be more dear or natural than sincere imitation of the Lord's prayer life. Frequent, heart-felt prayer characterized the life of Jesus. Though not explicitly stated, we believe that the forty days of fasting and temptation were also forty days of prayer (Luke 4). One reason for that belief is that prayer and fasting so often accompany one another in the New Testament (cf. Luke 2:37;

Matt 16:1–18). Another is that following the defeat of Satan, "Jesus returned in the power of the Spirit to Galilee ..." (Luke 4:14). We rightly associate prayer and spiritual power.

The gospel writers emphasize the fact that Jesus prayed before and during major ministry events. Luke 3:21–22 reports that Jesus prayed immediately after His baptism and that God was "well pleased" with both actions. Before choosing the twelve, "He went out to the mountain to pray, and continued all night in prayer to God" (Luke 6:12). Luke 22:39–46 describes Jesus's prayer in the garden on the night of His betrayal. John 17 documents His intercessory prayer for the disciples leading up to that night.

Scripture reminds us that prayer accompanied other special events in the life of Jesus. Jesus was not in the boat with the disciples as they faced a fearsome storm because "when He had sent them away, He departed to the mountain to pray" (Mark 6:46). The occasion of Peter's confession of Jesus as "The Christ of God" in Luke 9:18–20 begins with the disciples finding Jesus "as He was alone praying." Luke's account of the transfiguration is introduced with the words, "... He took Peter, John, and James and went up on the mountain to pray" (9:28).

Of the many labels Jesus could rightly wear, none would seem more fitting than Jesus Christ, Man of Prayer.

What an outstanding request! "Lord, teach us to

pray ..." (Luke 11:1) pulls back the curtain to reveal reasons for the appeal. Jesus was praying (again) in the presence of His disciples. We say "again" in light of Luke 5:16: "So He Himself often withdrew into the wilderness and prayed." The disciples knew from observation that prayer was important to Jesus. Mark 1:35 supports this truth: "Now in the morning, having arisen a long while before daylight, He went out and departed to a solitary place, and there He prayed."

Not only had the disciples observed the frequency of Jesus's prayers, they had also seen the fruit of His prayers. We think of Luke 9:10–17 where Jesus blessed the five loaves and two fish before breaking them into enough pieces to feed about 5,000—and with fragments left over. The miracle of healing in Luke 9:37–42 stands as another example. After the disciples could not cast out a demon afflicting a child, Jesus "healed the child, and gave him back to his father." The parallel account in Mark 9:28–29 shares the disciples' logical question, "Why could we not cast it out?" as well as Jesus's answer, "This kind can come out by nothing but prayer and fasting." We also think of Luke 18:1: "Then He spoke a parable to them, that men always ought to pray and not lose heart." Certainly, we think of Jesus praying from the cross (Luke 23:34, 46).

Luke 11:1 asserts that prayer is a practice and a discipline that can be taught and learned. The disciples of Jesus knew that John had taught his disciples to pray.

Prayer

They wanted similar instruction. Contrary to what some might expect today, Jesus obliged them. There was no chiding for needing instruction. There was no philosophical discourse on how prayer "just flows from the heart" and is "either spontaneous or not real." Rather, Jesus welcomed the opportunity to teach.

Entire books have been written about "The Lord's Prayer" or "The Model Prayer," usually from the fuller version found in Matthew 6:7–15. It would be foolish to assert that the model prayer is intended as a rigid script, the only prayer to be offered by any disciple of Christ. Scripture records other prayers of Christ and of disciples. Rather, the model prayer is exemplary.

- It is exemplary in its brevity. There is no need for "vain repetitions" or "many words" (Matt 6:7). Of course this fact needs to be balanced by the truth that Jesus Himself "continued all night in prayer" on occasion (Luke 6:12).
- It is exemplary in its simplicity. There is no specialized vocabulary; there are no complex philosophical issues.
- It is exemplary in its humility. God is the Father who rules from heaven. His name (not ours) is holy and to be uplifted. We exist to His glory and to do His will. We depend on Him for our daily bread. We are

morally, ethically, and spiritually responsible to Him. We dare not face temptation without His help.
- It is exemplary in its realism. Physical needs exist. We all sin and need God's forgiveness. Humans also sin against one another and must practice forgiveness. There is an "evil one" who opposes and will destroy us unless God effects deliverance.

Jesus's teaching on prayer from Luke 11 does not stop with verse 5; rather, it continues through verse 13. Jesus offers bonus teaching that encourages the constant practice of prayer. Even a friend, if disturbed at midnight, could be reluctant to help. That friend might need prodding. Not so with God: "For everyone who asks receives, and he who seeks finds, and to him who knocks it will be opened" (Luke 11:10).

Even the evil people of this world tend to give good gifts to family members and those they love. "If you then, being evil, know how to give good gifts to your children, how much more will your heavenly Father give the Holy Spirit to those who ask Him!" (Luke 11:13). God gives better than we ask because God knows better than we know and God loves better than we love.

Application

We are blessed when one of our first and most frequent prayers is the simple words of Luke 11:1: "Lord, teach us to pray." We can be helped tremendously by studying the prayer life of Jesus from the gospels.

In that Jesus was utterly respectful of what we call the Old Testament, we can also learn from the outstanding examples we find there. Think of Moses's prayers. Think of Hannah's prayer from 1 Sam 1. Think of Daniel's prayer life. Think of David's penitent prayer in Psalm 51.

In that "all Scripture is given by inspiration of God" (2 Tim 3:16), we can learn from the broader New Testament teaching on prayer. We remember aged Anna "who served God with fastings and prayers night and day" (Luke 2:37). There is Paul's constancy of prayer for the brethren (Col 1:3; 1 Thess 1:2; 2:13). We love the beautiful description of Epaphras, "always laboring fervently for you in prayers ..." (Col 4:12). And we take great comfort in the divine intercession and mediation that assist our prayers (Rom 8:26–28; 1 Tim 2:1–7; 1 John 2:1–2). God will not leave us alone in prayer.

Though no book compares to God's word, there is extensive literature on prayer that has proven helpful to many. From scholarly to devotional in nature, this literature can encourage our practice of biblical prayer. Some also benefit from keeping a prayer list, a prayer journal, or both.

In light of 1 Corinthians 1:11 and Philippians 3:17, we can also deepen and improve our prayer lives by noting the examples and soliciting the encouragement of brethren who have learned the heart and practice of prayer better than we. Sometimes we identify such men from their public prayers and teaching. Sometimes we identify such ladies from their rich comments during Bible class or their happy reports, "I want you to know that I pray for you and for the Lord's church every day."

Conclusion

We need to ask Jesus to teach us to pray because we can't be like Jesus unless we pray like Jesus. It's a simple statement with profound implications. It's a spiritual imperative that holds unimaginable blessings (Eph 4:11–16).

Discussion

1. Why and in what senses is it still wise for us to ask Jesus to teach us to pray?
2. In your best judgment, what are the most common errors Christians make in their prayer lives?
3. What are the key connections between

Prayer

praying like Jesus prayed and being "clothed in Christ"?

4. What keeps Christians from praying like Jesus prayed?

3. **LIVING IN SCRIPTURE**
NATHAN DAILY

Nehemiah 9:6–37

One Main Thing

Reciting the story of God instills the people of God with identity, purpose, and hope.

Introduction

The Bible is a daunting book. At first glance, these sixty-six books full of strange names, unfamiliar words, and ancient practices written in diverse cultural settings long ago and bound into a single volume that typically runs at least a few thousand pages can intimidate even the most curious and patient of readers. At the same time, God's people regard the biblical books as living Scripture and, thereby, continue to find purpose in life, meaning in monotony, and comfort in trouble within the pages of these old texts from ancient Israel and the early church. A primary way to begin to encounter and grasp the complexities of the Bible is through a model provided by ancient Israel and the early church themselves: reciting the story of God.

Readers do not encounter the Bible as a single story with a beginning, middle, and end. The books do not form a strict chronological scheme, and, often, they repeat events (e.g., Samuel–Kings and Chronicles or the Gospels). In fact, many of the books are not even narrative story but poetry, letter, law, proverb, and more. Rather, the Bible is a series of unique books, each telling its own story in its own way. It is within these unique books that biblical authors appeal to an underlying story. Summaries of this story are found throughout the Bible in several recitals of God's saving actions (Deut 6:20–25; 26:1–11; Josh 24:2–28; Neh 9:6–37; Ps 78; 105; 106; 135; 136; Acts 7:2–53; 13:16–41; Heb 11). These recitals highlight moments such as Creation, the call of Abraham, the life of Jacob, the Exodus, the gift of law at Sinai, the tragedy of the Babylonian Exile, and the death of Jesus. Through the memory of seminal moments from the past where God brought deliverance or enacted judgment, the believing community's recitation of the story invites imagination toward God's capability for action in the present.

Deuteronomy 6:20–24 envisions a child asking a

parent the meaning of God's laws for Israel. Throughout the book, Deuteronomy exhibits a concern for children understanding the law because there is always a next generation who must make decisions about life in relation to God (Deut 1:39; 4:9–10, 25; 11:1–19; 32:46). So, the parent must not answer the child with a simple "it is the law so we just do it" or even with a discussion of the particular law that generates the question. Rather, the parent should respond with a story. Here, as in the Ten Commandments (Exod 20:2; Deut 5:6), the story of the Exodus from Egypt provides definition for the laws that God gives to Israel. The laws of Deuteronomy simply will not make sense for future generations apart from the story of God's gracious salvation of the Israelites. The beginning of understanding or true education is grounded not in the imperative, "just do it because I said so," but in the indicative—the story of what God has already done.

Psalm 105 and 106 both present a recital citing many of God's acts of deliverance from the time of Abraham to the conquest of the land of Canaan. Even though both focus on God's past actions as a basis for praise (105:1–3, 45; 106:1–2, 47–48), the tone of each Psalm is very different. Whereas Psalm 105 almost exclusively presents God as the subject and is positive throughout (105:8–11; 24, 37, 39), Psalm 106 offers several of the same events to highlight human sins of the past (106:6–7, 13, 19–21, 24, etc.) in contrast to God's salvific action (106:8, 10) and covenantal fidelity (106:43–44). The story functionally offers itself as joyful praise (105) or as somber plea for forgiveness and deliverance (106).

Nehemiah 9:6–37 expresses the most detailed illustration of the recital of the story in the Bible. Beginning at creation and ending in the time of Nehemiah, the prayer recites many of the highs and lows encountered throughout the story of God (9:6–31). By beginning the final section of the prayer with the word "now" and ending with the words "we are in great distress" (9:32, 37), the story becomes a statement of faith. As the community shifts from recital of past event to present day trouble, readers realize that the community prays the story of God to (1) align themselves with the people of God from long ago and (2) express certainty that God can act again on behalf of this people. The community finds itself within a larger story and expects that its own situation can change because the story itself has taught the nature of God (9:31).

Acts 7 presents a speech by Stephen in the final moments of his life. By consistently speaking positively of God's action throughout history beginning with Abraham and carrying the story through the life, death, resurrection, and ascension of Jesus, Stephen refutes the charge of blasphemy (6:10–11) and shifts the charge toward his audience (7:51–53). Stephen does not directly defend himself during his speech. Rather, by reciting the story he aligns himself with those who accept the good God has done throughout history and witness to the vital role of the death of the innocent Righteous One within the story of God (7:52; cf. Luke 23:47; Acts 3:14).

Each of these examples presents a story visualizing a God who acts and remains faithful for the benefit of a people. The recitals are not history lessons but are claims by the faithful that God moves, reacts, and works. Knowing that the very core or nature of God is bound up with acting and doing provides great hope for God's people. Hearing and reciting the story of God provides the faithful community with a fertile starting point for understanding tradition, reflecting on its own place within the story, and expecting, no matter the situation, that God is the one capable of adding another chapter to the story.

Application

Christian identity hinges on recognizing God's action as primary gift and human reaction as secondary response (1 John 4:19). Therefore, the story of God informs and rearranges reality and imagination for those who know they are a part of the story.

Through encounter with text, the story of God shapes silence into speech. Many biblical books begin with images from the story of God so that readers will understand their current plight is encased within that

Living in Scripture

story (Matt 1:1–17; Mark 1:1–3; Luke 1:1; John 1:1–5; Acts 1:1; Rom 1:2; Gal 1:1–5; Jas 1:1; 1 Pet 1:1, 20). Similarly, even though the Bible is big and there is always more to learn, the Christian's speech has a beginning when infused with the outline of the story. The outline, found in Neh 9 or Acts 7, is not the end of Bible study. Rather, every encounter with a biblical text is an opportunity to gain greater clarity for retelling the story. Reciting the story of God is not a challenge to memorize the details of history or Bible trivia but an invitation to fullness and purpose within the Christian life afforded by grasping the significance of God's actions from Creation to the End (Gen 1:1; Ps 104; Rev 1:8; 22:13, 20).

Through practice of worship, the story of God shapes chaos into coherence. Worship is a powerful response from created toward creator when story saturates practice with meaning. The Lord's Supper practiced weekly without the story lacks purpose and could even be confusing. Fastened closely to the story, the Lord's Supper looks backward with memory and forward with anticipation, encapsulating the story in one visible act (1 Cor 11:26). Consistent practice of the story of God in worship enables Christians to regularly recite the story with others. Practice breeds coherence so that the story of God, rather than the competing chaotic stories heard throughout the week, has opportunity to consistently form the people of God.

Through repetition in life, the story of God shapes

despair into hope. The hope envisioned at the end of the story does not allow escape from the often painful reality of the present (Rev 21:3–4). However, time with text and worship facilitate the story's ability to impact ordinary demands of life. This repetition, stimulated by story and encountered in community, tends to open the eyes of the faithful, contradict stories of despair, and elicit speech and action from those who know they are in the story (Luke 24:30–35). Though the story never guarantees a life of ease, it does present God's people with potential for imagining each day from a new and hopeful perspective, the perspective of a God of covenant who, in fidelity, will bring the story to completion (Luke 24:30–35; Phil 1:6; Rev 22:20).

Conclusion

Through reciting the story, readers of the Bible understand themselves as players in an ongoing drama initiated and sustained by its primary character: the God of Abraham. Reciting the story functions as a bridge, for the community of faith, between foundational claims of Scripture and specifics of Christian practice. The story sparks the people of God to more clearly envision its own place within God's purpose and, thereby, desire to love, live in, speak of, and enact God's own vision for the world.

Discussion

1. Why do people like to tell stories?
2. Create a top-ten list of the acts of God in the Bible. Share your list with others. Discuss why the you chose these events. How were your choices easy or difficult? How does your list differ from that of others?
3. Why do so many recitals of the story of God include the promise to Abraham (Gen 12)?
4. Name several doctrines, teachings, or practices within your church community, and explain how each is more meaningful when understood in the context of the story of God.
5. Nehemiah 9:32–37 expresses the distress of Nehemiah's post-exilic community. If you prayed the story of God in Nehemiah 9, how would your community conclude the prayer? How does this passage fit your own church context? How is your context different? What issues do you currently face as a group?
6. Pick your favorite book of the Bible. How does this book relate to the broader story of God? Are there any specific verses, images, or themes within the book that directly rely on or relate to the story?

7. What stories or narratives does the world consistently tell that compete with the story of God? How can we make sure we are impacted by the story of God rather than the stories of the world?

4. BEING A SHEEP
PHILIP GOAD

1 Peter 5:5

One Main Thing

In order for the Lord to truly function as our shepherd, we must embrace the role of being His sheep.

Introduction

One of the great psalms of thanksgiving states, "Know that the Lord Himself is God; It is He who has made us, and not we ourselves; We are His people and the sheep of His pasture" (Ps 100:3). David begins the well-known Psalm 23 by stating, "The Lord is my shepherd." From Old Testament times, God has been referred to as a shepherd and His people as sheep.

Jesus incorporated this same metaphor into His ministry. In John 10:11, God the Son said, "I am the good shepherd; the good shepherd lays down His life for the sheep." Later in the New Testament, as the inspired pattern is revealed for leadership in the church, 1 Peter 5:2 used this metaphor when church elders are instructed to "shepherd" the flock.

And so, in both the Old and New Testaments, it is evident that people who intend to be in a relationship with God are referred to as sheep. But what does it mean to be sheep? Is it necessary to embrace this role?

Application

What does the Bible say about being a sheep?

In order to understand and embrace Christian living from the perspective of being a sheep, it is first important to be reminded of some characteristics of sheep. An online search for "characteristics of sheep" reveals that sheep are ...

- Fearful and easily panicked. They will run from what scares them and herd together for safety.
- Followers. They will typically follow the leader, even when it is not wise.
- Not very smart as animals go. They do not always discern well in choosing food or water.
- Social. They need to see other sheep around them.

From this brief list, it is easy to see why sheep depend so heavily on a shepherd. But does being referred to as a sheep sound like a good thing? Being compared to sheep, after all, is counter-cultural. People today are more educated than ever before, and with that education comes a high degree of self-reliance. In addition, our post-modern world has produced people who are highly skeptical, ready to challenge authority, and who live with the Burger King mentality. You probably remember the slogan, "Have it your way." In other words, culture promotes an independent, self-reliant mindset; not one of humbly having to depend on someone else.

The Importance of Humility

Developing a spirit of humility is a necessary first step in successfully embracing the role of a sheep. As 1 Peter concludes, chapter 5 begins with Peter sharing some instructions for shepherds. But then in verse 5, he turns his instruction to the sheep and, more broadly, to everyone. He states, "You younger men, likewise, be subject to your elders; and all of you, clothe yourselves with humility toward one another, for God is opposed to the proud, but gives grace to the humble." The following verse goes on to reveal that clothing oneself with humility is really to humble oneself before God!

It is worth noting that the command for sheep to be in

subjection to elders and for everyone to be clothed with humility is not stated with qualifiers. In others words, Peter does not provide a list of exceptions for times when this instruction can be ignored. It is further worth noting that humility is to flow in all directions. Verse 5 says, "and all of you, clothe yourself with humility toward one another ..." That means the entire body, both shepherds and sheep, are to operate with a spirit of humility.

Commenting on this section of 1 Peter, Duane Warden states,

> In order for elders to lead, there must be people who are willing to follow. If it is true that pride and arrogance are fundamental to an anti-God frame of mind, it follows that humility and submission are prerequisites for a God-approved frame of mind.[1]

This God-approved frame of mind is necessary if sheep are going to do obedience and subjection well.

Obedience and Subjection

Peter's instruction in 1 Peter 5:5 is for the younger men to "be subject to your elders." It is the idea that sheep are purposely and willfully placing themselves under the authority of church leadership. That may not always be easy, but it is the biblical plan.

The first part of Hebrews 13:17 states it this way:

"Obey your leaders and submit to them, for they keep watch over your souls as those who will give an account ..." This verse is powerful because, along with the instruction, it provides the reason for the command. Elders have been entrusted with a responsibility to shepherd the flock, and this verse indicates that they will give an account for the way in which they have fed, protected, and nurtured the sheep.

Notice that the second part of the verse expands the instruction being given to the sheep by saying, "Let them [elders/shepherds] do this [shepherd the flock] with joy and not with grief, for this would be unprofitable for you [sheep]." This part of the instruction calls every member of the body to self-examination with the question being, "As it relates to me, am I making the work of my shepherds a joy, or am I causing them grief?"

The Role of Trust

Obviously, sheep will follow a shepherd because there is a relationship of trust. Sheep recognize and trust the shepherd. In the church today, sheep must trust the shepherds that are leading the congregation. Elders are still human and, therefore, imperfect. However, when the church is diligent to install qualified men as shepherds (see 1 Tim 3 and Titus 1), and when these men shepherd according to the instructions provided in 1 Peter 5:1–3, a relationship should naturally result where sheep trust the shepherds.

Practical suggestions for being a "good" sheep:
Live in peace with one another.

How do we treat the people for whom we have great respect? In 1 Thessalonians 5:12–13, Paul answers this question. He writes,

> But we request of you brethren, that you appreciate those who diligently labor among you, and have charge over you in the Lord and give you instruction, and that you esteem them very highly in love because of their work. Live in peace with one another.

The instruction calls for sheep to assign high value to the shepherds. Paul is calling on the sheep to love the shepherds. He concludes by saying that one of the ways to demonstrate this is for sheep to get along peacefully with each other. Think about it: shepherds can more effectively focus on protecting the flock from outside threats when the sheep are at peace with each other.

So how can sheep succeed? What if each sheep could be less concerned about having his/her own way? How would that impact the flock? Everything discussed in this chapter is easy when sheep agree with each other and with the shepherds. But what needs to happen when a decision results in disagreement?

Disagree in a biblical way.

Even though having his/her own way should not be super important to a Christian, at some point there will be disagreement. In those hopefully brief moments, how should disagreement be handled? Following are some ideas that will bless those moments of disagreement:

- Avoid the temptation to just start talking to anyone who will listen. The temptation is to voice disagreement and to discuss the disagreeable situation with everyone around. This harms rather than helps—and it should be avoided—because, often, the information being spread may actually be misinformation. 2 Corinthians 12:20 is just one of the New Testament passages that condemns gossip.
- Have a conversation with the shepherds. Good and effective shepherding involves strong communication with the sheep. Shepherds who are leading well will have an open door for answering questions and communicating. If the disagreement is over a matter of opinion or expediency, most shepherds want the sheep to share

feedback. If there is a concern that the disagreement may be about something that is at odds with Scripture, the Matthew 18:15 aspect of taking a fault directly to a brother comes into play here.
- In the end, love and peacefully submit. Unless a decision has been made that is in violation of scripture (which should be re-verified through joint Bible study with the shepherds), sheep should love each other, the elders, and then peacefully submit. Shepherds have a great responsibility and are often operating with an overall knowledge of a situation (some of those things possibly not being appropriate to share) that leads to the decision being made. Again, sheep trusting their shepherds is so important.

Conclusion

The big question becomes, as a sheep, will I allow God, through the elders He has ordained, to lead me? Christians are, after all, the sheep of His pasture. It's a big question and eternity may well hang in the balance.

Discussion

1. What are some of the reasons that a Christian in the 21st century might have a difficult time embracing the idea of being a sheep?
2. Why are terms like "obedience" and "subjection" not always popular?
3. How could shepherds facilitate a more trusting mindset among the sheep?
4. What would be the impact both inside and outside of the church if every member could embrace the command to "live at peace with one another?"
5. Why is it often difficult to peacefully submit?

Endnotes

1. Duane Warden, *1&2 Peter and Jude,* Truth for Today Commentary (Searcy, AR: Resource Publications, 2009), 271.

5. FRUIT OF THE SPIRIT
RAY REYNOLDS

Galatians 5:22–23

One Main Thing

The natural work of God's Holy Spirit is to produce fruit in the life of a Christian.

Introduction

In the book of Galatians, the apostle Paul expresses the need for true, genuine faith in Christ. He also encourages the church to see the conflict between the works of the flesh (Gal 5:19–21) and the fruit of the Spirit (Gal 5:22–23). We must choose whether to feed our soul or our flesh. Paul provides a list of nine great characteristics of the Holy Spirit: "love, joy, peace, longsuffering, kindness, goodness, faithfulness, gentleness, self-control." The fruit of the Spirit can be divided into three main groups: (1) Bearing Fruit for God (love, joy, peace); (2) Bearing Fruit for Others (longsuffering, kindness, goodness); and (3) Bearing Fruit for Ourselves (faithfulness, gentleness, self-control). Let's consider these three groups.

Application

Bearing Fruit for God: Love, Joy, Peace

Love should be natural because God is love (1 John 4:8). It was His love that compelled Him to send Jesus to the cross (John 3:16; Rom 5:8; 1 John 3:16; 4:16). Several commandments teach us to love God, love one another, love our enemies, and love ourselves. God is a God of love. Therefore, He wants His children to have the spirit of love (John 13:34–35). Paul defines love to the Corinthians (1 Cor 13:1–13). Are you bearing the fruit of love?

Joy should be natural because God is joy (1 Tim 1:11). God has always been full of joy (Gen 1–2; Isa 62:5). Jesus came to help His disciples fill their cups to overflowing (John 15:11). We need to be joyful if we hope to win others to Christ. People need to see that godly living is the way to true happiness. Unfortunately, there are many "sour" Christians who fail to represent adequately the image of Jesus. Paul loved to talk about joy (Rom 15:13; Phil 1:2, 7; 4:4). Are you bearing the fruit of joy?

Peace should be natural because God is peace

(Rom 15:33). In the Sermon on the Mount, Jesus encouraged the people to be peacemakers (Matt 5:9). Satan loves to cause division, but God is not the author of confusion (1 Cor 14:33). He wants us to be united in mind and judgment (1 Cor 1:10). Christians should hate conflict.

We should seek to reconcile others and ourselves to God. Paul teaches on this elsewhere (Rom 16:20; 1 Thess 5:23–24; 2 Tim 2:22). Are you bearing the fruit of peace?

Bearing Fruit for Others: Longsuffering, Kindness, Goodness

Longsuffering should be natural because God is longsuffering (Rom 2:4). We may think of the patience of Job or Paul, but no one is more patient than God! As we strive for maturity, we need to let patience work in us (Jas 1:2–4). It is hard to suffer long, but looking to Jesus's great example can help us. Think about His temptation, His trials, and His death. When hardship comes our way, we need to be more like Jesus. We must stand fast in the Lord and learn to suffer for Christ (Col 1:9–12; 1 Tim 1:17). Are you bearing the fruit of longsuffering?

Kindness should be natural because God is kind (Eph 2:4–7). We are made in the likeness—kindness—of God (Gen 1:27). To be kind is to be like God in every sense of the word. To be kind to others around us means to be humane, sympathetic, and understanding

(Rom 2:3–4; 11:22; 12:10; Col 3:12–17). We should practice the golden rule and treat others like we want to be treated (Matt 7:12). Are you bearing the fruit of kindness?

Goodness should be natural because God is good (Jas 1:17). We remind ourselves that, "God is good all the time! All the time, God is good!" Paul teaches us that if we want to experience the goodness of God we have to walk with Him (Rom 15:14). As we walk with Him, He will teach us His ways. He will teach us how to be good, to walk in righteousness, and guide others to the path of life (Ps 25:8; 136; 2 Thess 1:11–12; Titus 3:4–5). Are you bearing the fruit of goodness?

Bearing Fruit for Ourselves: Faithfulness, Gentleness, Self-Control

Faithfulness should be natural because God is faithful (Rom 3:3). The Old Testament confirms God's faithfulness. He is faithful to keep His promises (Ps 145:13). God will never leave us or forsake us (Heb 13:5) and He will be with us always (Matt 28:20). However, we have to take the steps of faith that are necessary for salvation because these promises are for His children (Acts 2:37–39). Paul truly understood the need for faithfulness in the church (1 Cor 4:14–17; 2 Tim 2:2). Are you bearing the fruit of faithfulness?

Gentleness should be natural because God is gentle (2 Cor 10:1). Later in his writings, specifically in

Phil 4:5–7, Paul encourages us to make gentleness known to all of mankind. To be gentle means to practice humility (Rom 12:16). We cannot allow pride or jealousy to overwhelm us. Those are the ways of the world. Instead, we need to seek the mind of Christ (Phil 2:5). Jesus was meek, lowly, and humble (Matt 11:18–20). Are you bearing the fruit of gentleness?

Self-control should be natural because God has self-control (Eph 1:11–12). He is not tempted by evil (Jas 1:13). Paul was not afraid to speak about the need to control yourself (Acts 24:15; Rom 6:20–23; 1 Cor 7:5, 9; Titus 2:1–6). It is interesting that Paul ends with self-control, which is arguably the hardest virtue. This fruit also bring us back full-circle to the works of the flesh. We have an obvious choice to make. Are you bearing the fruit of self-control?

Conclusion

The natural work of God's Holy Spirit is to help us to bear similar characteristics to God, our Heavenly Father. We are His children, and we should be conforming to His image. When we are connected to Jesus the True Vine (John 15:1–8), it will produce natural fruit in our lives. Jesus is the source of all spiritual life (John 14:6). As we grow in Christ, we begin to bear fruit for God, for others, and for ourselves. This will be the evidence of a changed life.

Jesus encouraged His disciples to be the salt of the

earth, the light of the world, and a city on a hill (Matt 5:13–15). God chooses to use us, and our example, to bring glory to Him (Matt 5:16; Phil 2:15). The world, of course, will hate us and reject us. They abhor the wholesome fruit of the Spirit and the pure ideals of truth because they reject God. Instead, they seek after "adultery, fornication, uncleanness, lewdness, idolatry, sorcery, hatred, contentions, jealousies, outbursts of wrath, selfish ambitions, dissensions, heresies, envy, murders, drunkenness, revelries, and the like," which lead them further away from God (Gal 5:19–21). Those inside the kingdom of God refuse to follow the path of wickedness. We seek the straight and narrow road that leads to eternal life (Matt 7:13–14). Will you bear the fruit of the Holy Spirit?

Discussion

1. Why should Christians bear the fruit of the spirit? What is the purpose?
2. What are the differences between the works of the flesh and the fruit of the spirit? How can we contrast the two lists?
3. What are the connections between the fruit of the spirit and the characteristics of God? Why is this necessary to emphasize?
4. What is meant by the phrase "against such there is no law"? Explain.

6. WORSHIP
MATT HEUPEL

Hebrews 10:22–31

One Main Thing

Worship–what is it? How is it done? Why is it done? What does it accomplish? When we uncover the answers to these questions, our minds are opened to a whole new understanding of God and His plan for humanity.

Introduction

Many people see their worship to God in one of two ways. The first group sees their worship to God as somewhat of a payment plan. They view their worship as a way of slowly giving something back to God in the form of sacrificing their time and money. This type of

Worship

believer understands the huge debt we owe to Jesus for His sacrifice, but also understands that it is a debt that will never be fully repaid. However, with each opportunity to worship we reveal that we are making some effort to give back to the One who gave so much.

The second group sees their worship as an investment plan. This group understands the debt as being already paid by Jesus, now we are just making investments into His kingdom so we will be able to have our "Mansion Over the Hilltop." They see that each time they worship, they are making some type of deposit that will enable them to receive some future blessing from God. Let me assure you that both of these views of worship are faulty and neither of them offer a correct understanding of what worship is and why we worship. Worship isn't about our giving back and certainly not a way of seeking a return on our "investment."

Application

So what is worship? In the Old Testament, the Hebrew word for "worship" meant to "prostrate oneself" or to "bow down." The first time it was used was when Abraham bowed down to the three messengers who announced the birth of Isaac in Genesis 18:2. The word signified what was done when one came in contact with God. In the New Testament, there are a few Greek terms that we can translate as "worship," but the most often used is *proskuneo*, which is defined as "to make obeisance, do reverence to" or "to kiss." It is the word that Jesus uses when being tempted by Satan in Matthew 4:10, and the word that Jesus used in His discussion with the woman at the well in John 4:21-24 concerning worshipping in "spirit and in truth." Therefore, worship should not be something that we feel is payment for Christ's services or a deposit into a heavenly bank account; rather, more of a reaction to greatness.

Why should we worship? The first and foremost answer is that it was commanded by God in both the New and Old Testaments. I intentionally placed the New before the Old so that by going backwards, we should see the command as well as the necessity of expressing our reaction to God for His greatness. In the New Testament, we have the command to worship in several places. All throughout the New Testament, we see the command and the example of the early Christians to "gather together," "meet together," or "assemble yourselves together" on the first day of the week from the moment the church was established and continued throughout the spread of the church (Acts 2:42,46; 20:7; 1 Cor 11:18; 14:26-40; Heb 10:22-31). The emphasis is placed on believers coming, assembling, and meeting together not only with one another, but with God as well. In Acts 20:7, Luke tells us that when they gathered on the first day of the week, they broke bread. This act is what Paul calls the "Lord's Supper" in 1 Corinthians 11:20–29. The Lord's Supper (or "communion" as we have often referred to it) is our way of being joined with Christ as we partake of the body and the blood. Therefore, when we come together, we are not only assembling with each other, but with God as well.

Why is such an assembling, or communing with Christ so important? For a long time, we were separated from Christ. Since the events of Genesis 3, when man sinned in the Garden, he separated himself from God (Isa 59:1–2). God has sought to provide a way that would lead us back into His presence, so we can have the same communion that Adam had with God before the Fall. God's plan was set into motion for this reunion in Genesis 3:15 when He pronounced the coming of One (the Messiah) who would crush the head of the snake (Satan), a prediction called the *proto-evangelium* (the first telling of the gospel). God continued His plan though men like Seth, Enoch, Noah, and Abraham as he used them to establish what faith in Him looks like. He further continued His plan in Moses when He instructed the nation of Israel to build a place that would be considered His abode: the Tabernacle (Exod 15:17; 29:44–46). It was within that Tabernacle upon the Mercy Seat that God said, "I will meet with you" (Exod 25:22). This was not only God's way of reminding His people of His everlasting love and care for them, but also to provide a means by which God's people could express their reaction to that love and a way for it to be reciprocated by sacrifices and offerings. In Leviticus 23, God appointed certain days and feasts in which He commanded that His people come and be in His presence. This served as a pattern of God's plan to restore the connection that had been lost since Adam's fall.

As time passed, the Tabernacle became a long-lasting fixture in what became the Temple that was built in the days of Solomon. However, these buildings were never meant to serve as the permanent place that God's people were commanded to come and offer up their reaction to His greatness. The incarnation of Christ brought about God coming in the form of man (Jesus Christ) to give Himself as the ultimate sacrifice (Heb 7:27; 10:1–22) so that the lost connection could be restored. He replaced that earthly Temple with His body (John 2:20). Today, those who have been baptized into Christ, have "put on Christ" (Gal 3:26–27), making them part of the body of Christ. Therefore, when we are gathered together for the purpose of worship and communion with God during the Lord's Supper, we are symbolically reuniting the body of Christ and re-establishing our bond with God that sin has broken for so long. It has been God's plan all along that the connection between God and man be restored in the form of our assembling together upon the first day of the week.

But that isn't the only blessing of our worshipping together. There is something that happens when believers come together to worship. The writer of Hebrews reveals three by-products of our gathering together:

- *Draw Near to God.* When we come together to worship with a "true heart and full assurance of faith," we can "draw near" to the House of God (Heb 10:19–22). In our efforts to "draw near to God, He will draw near to you" (Jas 4:8). Therefore, when we "assemble" with a true heart we are not only inviting God to restore our relationship with Him, we are also making efforts to grow closer to Him each time.
- *Holdfast our Profession of Faith.* Our faith in Christ is based on His being the Son of God and that He is a "rewarder of them that diligently seek Him" (Heb 11:6). However, with the struggles that are common to Christians as we live in this world, it can be difficult to remain strong and continue to draw close to Him. That is why a continued reminder of His eternal love and unique message of salvation are necessary for Christians to hear. This reminder provides the worshipper something to hold onto when the storms of life attempt to break us down. It is imperative that we continue to be reminded of even the most rudimentary

of Biblical principles, so we do not allow ourselves to slip (Heb 2:1–3). When we assemble, we are strengthening our grip on our faith.

- *Encourage Others to Exercise Their Faith.* When Christians are assembled together to worship, there seems to be a dynamic between the "true worshippers." They become energized to be "provoked," or "aroused," to participate in things that promote "love and good works."

In commanding us to worship in a corporate way, God has granted us not only a way to get close to Him, but also a way to hold on to the faith we have and motivate others to do the same. If that were not enough of a reason to worship God, there remains another that needs to be discussed. To answer the question, "Why should we worship God?" I will defer to science. (Yes, I said science!) Newton's Third Law of Motion says, "For every action, there is an equal and opposite reaction." God's action of sending Christ to die for us requires a reaction on our part. God is not simply a force, nor is our reaction to His love near equal to the love that He has bestowed upon us. However, when a true believer begins to understand the gravity of God's love for them, they are compelled to worship. It just comes naturally. Over and over in God's Word, when someone comes in contact to the awesomeness of God, it is almost a reflex reaction to "prostrate oneself" or "make obeisance, or reverence" or "kiss." Isaiah and Paul both remind us that there will be a day when "every knee shall bow and every tongue will confess" the name of Jesus (Isa 45:25; Rom 14:11; Phil 2:10). Therefore, the answer to the question, "Why should we worship?" should be, "How can we not?!"

Conclusion

Worship is not about paying a debt or making an investment. It is more about the true believer wanting to grow closer to God every chance that he or she gets and then simply doing what comes naturally: bowing down to greatness!

Discussion

1. Discuss the impact of the sin in the Garden of Eden and the separation it caused between God and man.
2. Discuss how Christ bridges the gap between God and us.
3. What are some ways that being a part of the corporate worship service helps us "holdfast" to our faith?
4. What are some ways that being a part of the

corporate worship service helps us encourage others to exercise their faith?
5. Discuss different personal examples of how you felt closer to God after a worship service.

7. **SPIRITUAL DISCIPLINE**
ARVY DUPUY

2 Corinthians 5:17

One Main Thing

We act as if spiritual growth is automatic and comes without planning; it does not.

Introduction

The excitement that a newborn baby brings is unfathomable. Everyone—family, friends, even neighbors—get involved and, in time, emotionally invest in the precious little one. As the child grows and takes their first steps or says their first words, everyone joins in the celebration. But what happens if the child does not grow properly? What do you do if universally accepted developmental milestones are delayed or worse—never happen? The response is immediate and declarative. Grandparents panic. Parents rush the child to the doctor and demand answers. Why? Because physical growth is expected and if it does not happen, everyone knows that something is wrong.

Application

In 2 Corinthians 5:17, Paul tells us that when we are in Christ (Gal 3:27) we are a new creation. As new creatures, we are like newborn babies that naturally crave spiritual milk (1 Pet 2:2). However, there is an expectation that we will grow in the grace and knowledge of our Lord and Savior Jesus Christ (2 Pet 3:18). When this growth does not happen, problems ensue and things are out of order (Heb 5:12). There is a clear biblical mandate that spiritual growth and development is expected and is the norm. When that maturation process does not occur, we must understand that something is wrong. Furthermore, once we recognize something is not as it should be, we must be willing to find out why.

If growth is expected, how does that growth take place? In college, I had a professor who believed in what he called "classroom osmosis." He explained it this way: just show up to class, don't be late, don't disturb the other students, and I will give you five points on your final grade. He believed that by just showing up a student would learn something (i.e. through osmosis). I am not sure that is how it works,

Spiritual Discipline

but that is certainly how we have conducted business in churches for far too long. Once someone has professed Christ and been immersed into Him, too often we imply to them the only requirement moving forward is "just show up." If you do that, then everything will fall into place. We act as if spiritual growth is automatic and comes without planning or forethought; it does not.

There is no doubt that attendance is important. We should (and must) encourage and promote attendance at corporate worship and Bible classes. However, is that where real growth takes place? As important as all those times are, "spiritual osmosis" may not be all we sometimes credit it to be. In fact, the exact opposite is true. That is what the Hebrew writer is referencing in Hebrews 5:12 when he states, "For though by this time you ought to be teachers, you have need again for someone to teach you the elementary principles of the oracles of God, and you have come to need milk and not solid food." In verse 14 he continues, "solid food is for the mature, who because of practice have their senses trained to discern good and evil." In short, he calls them out not for poor attendance, but for a lack of spiritual growth. They should have developed to the point of solid food but were still on milk. Something had delayed and stunted their growth and the writer says this is wrong.

A survey of believers indicates that real growth and transformation takes place through the habit and practice of spiritual disciplines—disciplines lived out away from corporate worship and classes. Hawkins and Parkinson found that there are several primary areas that catalyze spiritual growth.[1] Organized church activities and spiritual beliefs are certainly among that list and vitally important. However, there are others—others that have far too long been ignored. These additional areas have significant, impact on spiritual growth.

The first is our willingness to talk to others about our faith. Many of you may have participated in an evangelism class at some time. How long ago has it been? When was the last time you have intentionally put forth the effort to improve your ability to share your faith? Are you prepared to step through the door of opportunity if it presents itself today to talk about Jesus to others? Like any skill, we must be prepared to use it. Practice and model your reaction and response to people in varying situations. Put thought and prayer into how you can respond when people say things to you that will allow the conversation to turn to Christ. How often do you pray about sharing your faith with others? Are you prepared at any moment or situation to talk about the Lord? Do your actions demonstrate a commitment to the Great Commission? Sharing our faith is a spiritual discipline that everyone should possess and practice.

What about spiritual activities with others? Research shows that believers who understand their

Spiritual Discipline

gifts and talents and are ready at a moment's notice to use them have a faith that is growing. True biblical service expects nothing in return; no thanks, no pats on the back or recognition, whether public or private. In fact, in Luke 14, Christ stated we should seek out those who can never repay us to serve. It is in meeting the needs of others that we find real purpose in our lives. We are most like Jesus when we serve others. Every day we must live with the expectation that God will use us to serve someone that day. Not only should we serve but we must be a force to encourage and facilitate others being involved in service.

Another Monday to Saturday discipline that is vital to spiritual growth is reflection on God's word. Daily Bible reading is important, but our actions in this area must go beyond simply reading words on a page and checking off the daily assignment. Scripture must be the guide for the way we act and think all the time. We must understand the Bible to be not only the word of God, but also a provision of His instructions for our daily walk that is applicable to us today. Our worldview should not just be merely shaped by Scripture but defined by it. When we do read, our approach should begin with prayer—asking God to reveal truth to us and expose any areas of our lives that need to change. Approach the Bible with the expectation to discover a truth for daily living. When we finish reading, we might pray again, asking God to let us meditate on what we have just read so we may look for opportunities to apply it.

Prayer is also critical to cultivate spiritual depth in us. For most people who pray, their prayers are focused on themselves. In fact, respondents in a recent survey said they typically pray for their families and friends, along with praying for their needs, far more than anything or anyone else.[2] This anthropocentric approach to our prayer life mirrors how we live. What if we could shift our focus? What if we could pray to discover God's will more than expressing our own needs? Do we trust God to answer us when we pray and wait patiently for those answers in His time, not ours? Sadly, far too many believers expect growth in their prayer life but never intentionally seek ways to improve. Then there is balance—spending as much time talking to God as we do listening to Him. An active, vibrant prayer life includes thanksgiving, praise, and confession along with requests. Are we guilty of focusing only on one area to the exclusion of the others? If we believe the words of James 5:16, do our lives reflect a belief that our prayers impact our life and the lives of others? Certainly daily prayer is important, just as important is our approach and attitude to time communing with God. It is in our orison to the Father that we live out our complete dependence on Him.

G.K. Chesterton is credited with saying, "Just going to church does not make you Christian any more than standing in your garage makes you a car." So it is that just showing up, hoping upon hope that through osmosis, spiritual growth will take place and we will evolve into the follower of Jesus we are called to be. Attendance is important. However, it cannot stand alone as the sole source of development. If the words of the Hebrew writer urging us to "press on to maturity," (Heb 6:1) are to become real to us, then we must adopt and integrate spiritual disciplines into our lives.

Conclusion

It is time that we hold ourselves and others accountable. It is time that leadership clearly articulates an expectation that growth will happen and set in place structures that will facilitate this growth. It is time that those who have been on milk for far too long, move on to solid food. It is time for us to be the body that God intended for us to be: alive, active, and always growing.

Discussion

1. Have you ever had a class on spiritual growth?
2. Why do you think this topic is not discussed more often?
3. Compare reading Scripture and meditating on Scripture.
4. How would you explain the church's

allowance of long-time Christians being infants in the faith?
5. What is the difference between hoping God will use us in His kingdom and expecting it?
6. Explain how best to maintain an attitude of prayer throughout the day.
7. What is the similarity between spiritual growth and conforming to the image of Christ?
8. Contrast leadership that holds members responsible and those that do not. What does that convey to the membership?
9. What is the importance of having a prayer life that includes praise and thanksgiving?

Endnotes

1. Greg L. Hawkins, and Cally Parkinson, *Move: What 1,000 Churches Reveal about Spiritual Growth* (Grand Rapids, MI: Zondervan, 2011), 107.

2. Bob Smietana, LifeWayResearch.com: 2014.

8. EVANGELISM
JEREMY BARRIER

Matthew 28:18–20

One Main Thing

Christians are people who have the good news of God!

Introduction

"Mom, I've got good news to tell you! We're going to have a boy!" It is hard to explain what an exciting, exhilarating feeling it is that rushes through your body as these words are spoken. As a father of two children, it gave me unbelievable joy to call my mother and share the good news that we were going to have a child! Our son was born first, followed by our daughter, and in both cases, the excitement of telling friends and family was beyond words. I think of the tingling in my back, as the hairs stood up on my neck. I think of how I became weak in the knees with pleasure and anticipation. I think of the months of planning and joy that were experienced as we prepared to usher in the coming of a new family member, full of life, excitement, and all of the other emotions associated with such an adventure in life. Such is the Good News of Christ! In Mattew 28, when Jesus was standing there with the eleven remaining disciples, it was good news on their tongues that would fill their audiences with joy and excitement. When Paul said, in Romans 1:16, "I am not ashamed of the gospel," it was because he realized that he had such good news that could not be contained, and would certainly bring days, months, and years of joy to those who heard it!

If you are turning in your Bibles to Matthew 28 for the first time, I hate to tell you that these are the last three verses of the gospel. The word "gospel," meaning good news, has already been told and here you are catching the aftermath of the events as Jesus sends out His disciples to go on a bigger, greater, more extensive mission outside the borders of Palestine to the entire world. Nevertheless, so much is said in just these few words of Matthew 28. Jesus has already died. He has already risen from the grave and walks again. Judas is gone, and Peter has returned. The disciples have failed Him, and have swallowed their pride (at least 11 of them did). They are broken, but not destroyed; "persecuted, but not forsaken; perplexed, but not driven to despair." Here

Evangelism

in these final passages, Jesus is sending them out to tell the world that God had such a deep passion for us, that he was moved in His heart to come here in the form of Jesus, as a human, and attempt to connect with us. God desired to be with us. He wants to dine with us, get to know us, and spend his time with us. Wow!

Matthew 28:18–20 reads as follows:

> And Jesus came and spake unto them, saying, "All power is given unto me in heaven and in earth. Go ye therefore, and teach all nations, baptizing them in the name of the Father, and of the Son, and of the Holy Ghost: Teaching them to observe all things whatsoever I have commanded you: and, lo, I am with you always, even unto the end of the world." Amen.

First, a statement of autonomy and authority is made: "Listen to me, because the buck stops here." In essence, Jesus has the authority of the creator of the cosmos, and this authority extends outside the borders of the heavens even throughout the domains and kingdoms of this earth. With this in mind, Jesus is sending out these disciples to do three basic things: "Make disciples" as you go! It is assumed that Christians will be coming and going throughout the world, and as they go they should wear their faith on their sleeves. It should be within us through and through, that God has offered a message of hope and love to humanity that will bless everyone who hears.

Second, Jesus tells them that as they move in and out throughout all of the nations of the world, there will be people who hear, understand, and excitedly respond to the good news of God! When this happens, assist them in responding to God's great offer: immerse them in the name of the Father, the Son, and the Holy Spirit, so that they will be bathed in God, through and through, for a life filled with God's love for God's love.

Last, but not least, Jesus realized that even after we have heard the message of trust, hope, and steadfast compassion, many times it is extremely difficult to figure out how this should be done day in and day out. Thus, the disciples were commended to be involved in "teaching them to observe everything" that the disciples had witnessed in the life of Jesus. They had been with the Lord. They knew the Lord. They could pass on the stories of the Lord for the benefit of others who wanted to model their lives after the example of the Messiah.

Application

On various occasions, in over 30 different countries, and on five continents I have preached the good news of the coming of Jesus, the life of Jesus, the death of Jesus, and the resurrection of Jesus. In many instances, I have seen the "light bulb" in people's mind. I have

Evangelism

seen them bow their head in tears when they hear of the crucifixion. I have seen them weep with joy as the message of hope rung from the walls of the mud huts in Africa, "He has RISEN!" The message of Jesus is a message of overcoming. It is the story of overcoming impossible odds. It is a story that says, "Yes, the universe has design, it has a point, and it is God, and YES, He knows you and cares for you!" It is a message that tells us to believe and trust in other people after we have been burned and hurt by them time and again. It is a message that tells us we can still love, when people seem unlovable. The message of Jesus is the impossible made possible. It is the miraculous, awe-inspiring story that encourages me to get up each and every day. I am encouraged to do the next right thing. I am transfixed on rising from my bed, even when everything in my life says, "Give up." I will rise, because He rose. I will come forth and face the day, because He came forth and faced the day. What a message!

Discussion

1. Describe a time in your life when you had good news to share with someone you loved.
2. Why is the Good News of God good news?
3. Why was it important for Jesus to make sure

the disciples understand that He had "all authority in heaven and earth"?
4. What were the three things that Jesus told His disciples in Matthew 28:19–20?
5. Compare/contrast the three things Jesus told His disciples and explain how these things will help people who are coming to Christ for the first time.

9. MENTORING
BRAD MCKINNON

Matthew 12:49–50

One Main Thing

The ministry of Jesus is synonymous with the concept of discipling, and Jesus intended for that ministry to continue through His people by their mentoring of others.

Introduction

By nature, Christianity is a social experience. Brother, sister, mother, and father were ways Jesus thought about the relationship between God, Himself, and His disciples—"And pointing to his disciples, he said, 'Here are my mother and my brothers! For whoever does the will of my Father in heaven is my brother and sister and mother'" (Matt 12:49–50 NRSV). In addition to these typical familial terms, the New Testament also describes the association between Jesus and his followers as that of a teacher with His disciples. In fact, this is probably the most popular way the gospel writers characterized the partnership.

Talk of discipling or mentoring has been a trendy topic within pop theology over the last couple of decades or so. However, the notion of mentoring is not a new idea. It wasn't unfamiliar to ancient peoples in either religious or secular contexts. The name for the concept is derived from Homer's poem, *The Odyssey*. In the epic, as Odysseus leaves home to assume command in the Trojan War, he places his young son in the care of a friend named Mentor. Accordingly, the term "mentor" has come to mean an experienced and trusted advisor. A guide, guru, or consultant are other terms that come to mind. In New Testament language, you might say, "teacher." And, a teacher naturally has students or disciples. I remember my Latin teacher in high school beginning class each morning with the greeting, "Salvete, discipuli!" Or, "Hello, students!" Disciples are students. Students are disciples.

The goal of the teacher-disciple dynamic in Scripture is imitation. As Jesus once observed, "A disciple is not above the teacher, but everyone who is fully qualified will be like the teacher" (Luke 6:40). Reflecting on this sentiment, famed twentieth-century theologian Dietrich Bonhoeffer noted, "It is only because he became like us that we can become like him." This tells us what we already know: Jesus's ministry, as well as the group of followers His ministry created, was highly relational. In fact, the concept is practically indistinguishable from the ministry of Jesus itself. Consider three instances in Jesus's ministry that highlight the role of discipling in His work.

Matthew 5:1–16

Early in the Gospel of Matthew, we see Jesus as a teacher, but much more than a teacher. The context of the Sermon on the Mount seems to be the immediate days after calling His first disciples (Matt 4:18–22). "Follow me," Jesus said simply to Simon, Andrew, James, and John—owners of a fledgling fishing business. "I'm doing something new and amazing, and you'll want to be a part of it." As He begins rehearsing what we've come to know as the Beatitudes, the disciples begin to understand that Jesus really is doing something revolutionary. He's not so much setting conditions for blessing, rather He's reassuring those who actually are poor, sad, hungry, and persecuted that there is hope. I've come to bring a blessing. You already are the salt of the earth. You are the light of the world. Just be sure to act that way. As mentor, Jesus helped His followers understand not just their potential, but He introduced them to who they already were. There would be no place for marginalization in Jesus's kingdom. Everyone was important and needed.

Matthew 9:9–13

Jesus's ability to see what others could not see, even in themselves, is highlighted by the call of Matthew. Jesus sees Matthew at work collecting taxes, and he again simply invites the prospect: "Follow me." I assume Matthew and Jesus had already had some kind of previous interaction with each other, but I'm sure Matthew, a Jew working in collaboration with Roman occupiers, wasn't an obvious choice to be one of Jesus's followers. Two things stand out in this passage. First, Jesus was evidently looking for additional followers. When He observes Matthew, Matthew immediately gets the call. Jesus had things to do and places to go and needed or at least wanted help. Matthew's responsibility was simply to tag along, observe, and learn. Second, Jesus wasn't choosing those who seemingly had it all together or who could win a popularity contest. He had a longer view in mind.

Matthew 10:5–15

Eventually, the disciples were ready to begin venturing out a little on their own. Before they set out, Jesus wanted them to understand a few things. First, they were part of a community. So, Jesus talks about Israel, the kingdom of heaven, as well as homes and villages where they might be received hospitably.

Second, they could accomplish more than they could possibly imagine at this point. Jesus anticipates their curing the sick, raising the dead, cleansing lepers, and casting out demons. Third, with all of these good works to do, it was all hands on deck. Jesus couldn't help but multiply Himself, because there was so much that needed to be done.

Application

Good Morning, Students

For mentors, it's important to recognize that God has already qualified each believer for discipleship. Looking out at the ragtag group of early disciples, Jesus couldn't have been very impressed. But, Jesus saw beyond appearances to something much deeper. To be good mentors, experienced believers must recognize the inherent value in even the most unsophisticated Christian. In fact, that lack of sophistication may very well be what enables someone to embody the gospel most effectively. Having the ability to make everyone feel included is a vital mentoring skill.

With Eyes Wide Open

For a mentoring relationship to develop, there must be observation in both directions—from teacher to potential student and from student to future teacher. The advanced believer must consider those who might benefit from such a relationship, just as Jesus observed Matthew at the tax booth. These prospects aren't always obvious. Good leaders see latent qualities in others—not just who they are at any one moment in time, but who they can be with a little help. Taking the long view when dealing with people requires patience, but it's well worth it. For those who are just beginning to develop their faith, it's necessary to be prepared to receive guidance and mentoring too. When given the opportunity to follow Jesus, Matthew didn't hesitate. We shouldn't overlook opportunities to learn from those more mature in the faith.

The Laborers are Few

It is sometimes tempting to see ministry as a one-person show. However, there is so much to accomplish that we can't afford to dismiss any willing participant. Acknowledging the church as a community allows us to accomplish so much more than we could possibly achieve on our own. The image of community underscores individual strengths and downplays personal weaknesses. This, in turn, breeds confidence that blesses others.

Conclusion

After His resurrection, Jesus seemed focused on leaving a legacy by preparing His current followers to replicate themselves through mentorship or discipleship. What were His disciples to do going forward? The same thing Jesus Himself had been doing all these years—"Go therefore and make disciples" (Matt 28:19).

As I think about mentoring as a tool for leaving a legacy, I'm reminded of an old Chinese proverb, roughly translated:

> Not having heard something is not as good as having heard it; having heard it is not as good as having seen it; having seen it is not as good as knowing it; knowing it is not as good as putting it into practice.

Condensed, you get something like the popular quotation: "Tell me and I forget, teach me and I may remember, involve me and I learn." No matter what you call it (involvement, mentoring, or discipleship), the idea of learning through observed practice is indispensable to the human experience in general and to the Christian life in particular.

Discussion

1. What do you think Jesus was suggesting by characterizing His early followers as the "salt of the earth" and "light of the world," just as His ministry was getting started?

2. What is the theological, cultural, social, and political significance of Jesus's choice of a tax collector to be one of His earliest disciples?
3. Before they even understood their own capabilities, Jesus had confidence in all that His disciples could and would accomplish. Why is this meaningful?
4. How can leaders today demonstrate the value they see in each team member regardless of one's experience or inexperience?
5. In what ways would taking the "longer view" in our relationships positively influence those we're trying to inspire?
6. How important is it that leaders demonstrate confidence in their followers? What are some practical steps mentors can take to help boost morale in others?

10. AUTHORITY
C. WAYNE KILPATRICK

JOHN 5:26–27

One Main Thing

To be clothed in Christ necessitates being clothed in the manner He has prescribed, by His directions, by His authority.

Introduction

Authority is defined as "having dominion, power, rule, or right over; to reign over; to have strength or power over; to have command over."

In the English language, one cannot say the words "authoritarian," "authoritative," "authority," "authorize," or "authorship" without reflecting upon the originator, creator, author of an idea, law, or concept. The word "author" is solidly embedded in each of these words. This binds the author and the author's original intent together as one—inseparable.

If one follows a concept, law, or idea meticulously, he or she must be in agreement with the originator or author of that concept, idea, or law. Therefore, when one claims biblical authority in a spiritual matter, he or she is claiming to be in agreement with the author's or originator's original intent or his authority.

The New Testament Scriptures emphasize the authority of Christ and His Father time and time again. Matthew 15: 6–9 shows the futility of human-originated authority in worship toward God. Human authority is in vain, useless, worthless. John 5:25–30 reveals that Christ has power over death and the grave. Matthew 17:1–8 stresses the authority of Christ, even above that of the Law of Moses and the Prophets. "This is my beloved Son, in whom I am well pleased, hear ye Him." Hebrews 1:1–2 tells us that God, by Christ, "made the worlds." That gives Christ authority over all the creation. By Him all things consist or are held together. Colossians 1:10–18 demonstrates that Christ is the creator of the world, creator of the church, and is head over the church—the authority. He is the authority in all spiritual matters—the only authority.

Paul tells us that Christ will keep this power and authority until death is destroyed. In 1 Corinthians 15: 23–28 Paul explains the sequence of the resurrection of the dead:

But every man in his own order: Christ the first fruits; afterward they that are Christ's at His coming. Then cometh the end, when He shall have delivered up the kingdom to God, even the Father; when He shall have put down all rule and all authority and power. For He must reign, till He hath put all enemies under His feet. The last enemy that shall be destroyed is death. For He hath put all things under His feet. But when He saith all things are put under Him, it is manifest that He is excepted, which did put all things under Him. And when all things shall be subdued unto Him, then shall the Son also Himself be subject unto Him that put all things under Him, that God may be all in all.

Therefore, as long as the earth stands, Christ is our authority in all spiritual matters. In order to be clothed in Christ we must follow His authority.

Our clothing can reveal a lot about who we are. It may reveal that we are poor, middle class, or wealthy. It may reveal that we are military, a farmer, an office worker, or a policeman. Because many things can be revealed by the clothing we wear, we must be careful that we do not send the wrong signal about ourselves. When we profess to be clothed in Christ we should be clothed the way He desires us to be dressed. That is, we must be dressed through or by the authority of Christ. To claim that we are dressed or clothed in Christ says to the world that we are trying to be Christ-like. If we desire to be Christ-like, then we must be willing to submit to that authority the only comes through our total commitment to Him.

Alexander the Great, one of the greatest military generals who ever lived, conquered almost the entire known world with his vast army. One night during a campaign, he couldn't sleep and left his tent to walk around the campgrounds.

As he was walking he came across a soldier asleep on guard duty—a serious offense. The penalty for falling asleep on guard duty was death; the soldier began to wake up as Alexander approached him. Recognizing who was standing in front of him, the young man feared for his life. "Do you know what the penalty is for falling asleep on guard duty?" Alexander the Great asked the soldier. "Yes, sir," the soldier responded in a quivering voice.

Alexander asked the soldier his name. The young man answered, "My name is Alexander, sir." Alexander repeated the question two more times and received the same answer from the young soldier. Alexander told the young man, "Soldier, either change your name or change your ways."

Alexander had the authority to bring instant death upon the young negligent soldier. For some reason he opted to forego the death penalty and give the soldier a second chance. Alexander had the authority to do as he wished. Christ has that very same authority. He will use all options on judgment day. Just as

Alexander told the young soldier to change his name or ways, Jesus says those who claim to be clothed in Christ but are not living right should stop using the name Christian or change their ways. Those who wear the name falsely are hypocrites and their end is not pretty. Jesus graphically describes what a master will do to his wicked slave: "And shall cut him asunder, and appoint him his portion with the hypocrites: there shall be weeping and gnashing of teeth" (Matt 24:51).

Application

All of our spiritual blessings come to us through Christ when we do everything by or through His authority: "And whatsoever ye do in word or deed, do all in the name of the Lord Jesus, giving thanks to God and the Father by Him" (Col 3:17).

We unite with Christ upon our baptism. "For ye are all the children of God by faith in Christ Jesus. For as many of you as have been baptized into Christ have put on Christ" (Gal 3:26–27). Therefore, everyone who has submitted to the authority of Christ, through faith and baptism, has put on Christ in His body, in His church (Eph 1:22–23). By being in the body of Christ—to whom "all power [authority] is given" (Matt 28:18)—we receive spiritual blessings (Col 3:24). If we are called the servants of the Lord Jesus, it is because we have been clothed by the authority of Christ. We have submitted to the authority of Christ, totally, in all things whether "in word or deed."

Everyone who has put on Christ has done so by trusting in the authority of Christ and believing in what He has done for us. We have been called to put on Christ, which means that we are to imitate Christ in every way to the best of our ability. That means to fully submit to His authority.

So to be fully clothed in Christ, we must be clothed through and by His authority. This enables us to look forward to that day when we will be clothed in immortality by the authority of Jesus Christ our Lord and Redeemer.

Discussion

1. Who has all power and authority?
2. Why is it important for a savior to have all power and authority?
3. How can a command mean anything without authority behind it?
4. Why is it crucial to be clothed by the authority of Christ?
5. What is suggested by wearing someone's name?
6. Would Christ be pleased with anyone who professes to wear His name and but does not try to live like Him?

11. DYING TO SIN
JUSTIN GUIN

Acts 2:38 & Romans 6:11

One Main Thing

The Christian is dead to sin and alive to God through Jesus Christ.

Introduction

The Christian and Identity

Every person struggles with sin. Most of us can quote Romans 3:23: "all have sinned and fallen short of God's glory." Even though sin affects our life, we must not allow it to become our master. Paul challenges us in Romans 6:11 (ESV): "So you also must consider yourselves dead to sin and alive to God in Christ Jesus." Our lives focus upon living under Christ's lordship because of his redemptive work at Calvary. We need both a master and savior. In our obedience to the gospel, two responses point to this principle. First, repentance demonstrates a change of thought and behavior. Second, baptism forgives ours sins and creates a new identity. Our new life demands lifestyle changes. These changes begin with repentance.

Application

Repentance and the Direction of a Christian's Life

One step in our conversion is repentance. When Peter preached the gospel in its fullness, it demanded a response, namely a change of life. In Acts 2, Peter concluded his sermon with one point, "God has made him both Lord and Christ, this Jesus whom you crucified" (v. 36). When the crowds heard it, they were "cut to the heart" (v. 37). What must they do to be saved from their sinful, murderous choice? Peter replied, "Repent and be baptized every one of you in the name of Jesus Christ, for the forgiveness of sins, and you will receive the gift of the Holy Spirit" (v. 38). Turn away from sin and be immersed in the name of Christ for the forgiveness of your sins. This decision created a new identity and lifestyle (2:42–47). Consistently in Acts, when the gospel is preached, repentance is demanded (Acts 3:17–21; 17:30–31; 20:21; 26:20). Why is repentance necessary in conversion?

Repentance means to change one's life as a result of a complete change of thought and attitude regarding sin and righteousness. In English, "repent" refers to contrition, a sorrowful emotion because of sinful choices. In Greek, it refers to a change in thought and behavior.[1] In 2 Corinthians 7:9-10, both contrition and change of behavior are in view. Paul wrote, "For godly grief produces a repentance that leads to salvation without regret, whereas worldly grief produces death" (2 Cor 7:10, ESV). Godly grief differs from worldly grief in a few ways. First, the source of the grief is different. Godly grief is caused by sin. Worldly grief is self-centered and is caused by a loss or denial of something we want for ourselves. Second, the result of godly grief is repentance and salvation. It moves one to action and change. Worldly grief leads to despair and has no spiritual benefit.[2]

Consider two examples of grief caused by a sinful choice, which produced different outcomes. First, consider Judas. Motivated by greed, he betrayed Jesus for 30 pieces of silver. Later, he regretted it and returned the money (Matt 27:5). Instead of repenting, his grief led to destruction. Next, consider Peter. He denied Jesus three times (Luke 22:54-62). Even though he made a terrible decision, he did not allow this to destroy him. Instead, he repented and became the leader Jesus needed him to be (John 21:15-21). The difference between the two apostles is repentance.

Feeling sorrow over sin is not repentance. Repentance is a change of thought and behavior.

Baptism and Putting on Christ

Peter issued a second command in response to the crowd's question: they must be baptized (Acts 2:38). Baptism was not a new practice. The Jews practiced immersion of proselytes, which signified a ritual cleansing and conversion. John the Baptist preached a "baptism of repentance for the forgiveness of sins" in preparation for the coming Messiah (Mark 1:4–5; cf. Act 19:4). Jesus submitted to baptism to fulfill all righteousness (Matt 3:15), and He and His disciples baptized those who followed Him (John 3:22, 26). Before His ascension, Jesus commanded His apostles to "make disciples" by teaching and baptizing others (Matt 28:19). So, Peter's command to submit to baptism was not something unfamiliar to the crowds. But, it was very different. Peter commanded them to be baptized "in the name of Jesus Christ" (Acts 2:38). This indicates they acknowledged their faith in Christ, accepted the terms of Peter's sermon, and changed their allegiance to serve Christ as their Lord.[3] Consequently, their sins were forgiven and they were added to the number of the disciples (2:47).

Baptism results in many different things in the life of a Christian. At conversion, baptism:

- Results in the forgiveness of sins (Acts 2:38; 22:16).
- Buries you with Christ, crucifies the old man, and raises you to walk in newness of life (Rom 6:1–7).
- Adds you to the body of Christ (1 Cor 12:13).
- Clothes you with Christ (Gal 3:27).
- Removes sin by the powerful working of God (Col 2:11–12).
- Saves you through the resurrection of Jesus Christ (1 Pet 3:21).

Furthermore, when the gospel is preached baptism is required at conversion (cf. Acts 8:12, 38; 10:47; 16:14–15; 22:16). These factors demonstrate the powerful "proclamation" baptism makes in a Christian's life. Putting on Christ creates a new identity and demands a new lifestyle.

Repentance and Baptism:
 Dying to Sin and Living for Christ
When we obey the gospel, the grace of God sets us free from sin and its consequences (Rom 6:17–18). We no longer serve self but are committed to becoming a "slave of righteousness." Repentance is the change of direction (Eph 4:17–24). It is the decision to turn toward away from sin and toward God.[4] Baptism forgives us of

our sins, and we are raised to walk in "newness" of life. After our conversion, the gospel requires us to live faithful, godly lives. We die to sin and live for Christ (Rom 6:11). What are some biblical principles, which will help us "walk in newness of life?"

First, we must realize a change in identity also changes our allegiance. Paul stated in Galatians 2:20,

> I have been crucified with Christ. It is no longer I who live, but Christ who lives in me. And the life I now live in the flesh I live by faith in the Son of God, who loved me and gave himself for me (Gal 2:20).

In this passage, Paul asserts a Christian must give complete allegiance to Jesus. Christ is not only my Savior but also my Master. The world begins to see Christ in us. After all, we are identified as Christians.

Second, we must no longer allow sin to control our lives. Sin will reign over us if we allow it, and it is a terrible master. We must consider ourselves dead to sin and alive to God through Jesus Christ (Rom 6:11). In Romans 6:12–23, Paul applies this principle to a Christian's life. Dying to sin requires life changes such as:

- Not obeying sin and its passions (v. 12)
- Not presenting ourselves "instruments" of unrighteousness (v.13).
- Becoming a slave of righteousness (v. 17–18).

- Striving to bear fruit, which leads to sanctification and eternal life (v. 19, 22).

We cannot take part in "unfruitful works of darkness." Instead, our lives must expose them through our obedience to Christ.

Third, we must imitate God's character in our daily walk with him. In 1 John 1, the apostle describes God as "light" who cannot fellowship with darkness in any way (v. 5). We cannot live in sin and claim to be walking with God (v. 6). John challenges us to "walk in the light." This produces two blessings in our lives:

- We have fellowship with God (v. 7a).
- Christ's blood continually cleanses us from all unrighteousness (v. 7b).

We will not always choose light over darkness. Sin is a struggle. When we do give in to temptation, he is faithful and just to forgive us as we confess our failures to him (1:9). He is a gracious God who is just and justifier of those who obey him (Rom 3:24–25).

Conclusion

Every person desires a savior, but few people want a lord and master. A Christian needs both. Becoming a Christian not only forgives our sins, but it also demands changes to our lifestyle. We are dead to sin and alive to God through Christ (Rom 6:11). Satan has made it his mission to divert us from the path that follows God's will. His tactics can be defeated. God provides the strength we need to live faithfully (Eph 6:10). He provides the resources we need, but the decision is ours to make. Will we live for Christ? Or, will we live for self? If we have died to sin, we will choose Christ.

Discussion

1. What is the importance of understanding Rom 6:11?
2. What is the difference between contrition and repentance? How do the examples of Peter and Judas help us understand this difference?
3. How does repentance prove we have made the decision to die to sin?
4. What is the connection between baptism and a new identity?
5. How can sin have dominion over us if we allow it to do so?

Endnotes

1. Johannes P. Louw and Eugene A. Nida, μετανοέω, μετάνοια, *Greek-English Lexicon of the New Testament Based on Semantic Domains,* 1:509.

2. David E. Garland, *2 Corinthians*, NAC 29 (Nashville: Broadman and Holman, 1999), 355.

3. David Roper, *Acts 1-14* (Searcy, AR: Resource Publications, 2002), 83.

4. J. Goetzmann, "Conversion", *NIDNTT* 1:354-59.

12. CHURCH INVOLVEMENT
LUCAS SUDDRETH

Matthew 25:14–30

One Main Thing

Being involved in the church is like being married. How are you going to get to know your spouse if you are never around?

Introduction

Perhaps you have heard stories of the lady down the street who lost her son in a car accident; the man who lost his wife to cancer; or the student struggling with addiction. These are common stories that break our hearts. We may think otherwise, but there are people in our very own churches, sitting in the pew right beside us, who are struggling, battling against various influences. These hurting people often feel alone, but as the mixed martial artist Conor McGregor said, "If one of us goes to war, we all go to war!" We can look to our own selves as proof of this. When one body part develops cancer, the whole body reacts. Similarly, this reasoning can be used within the church. Romans 12:4–5 states,

> For as in one body we have many members, and the members do not all have the same function, so we, though many, are one body in Christ, and *individually members one of another*.

Because we are all members of the same body, and members of one another, we must support one another. When one of us hurts, we all hurt.

Sadly, when facing pain and suffering, a member will typically hide one's self from others, isolate, and disassociate from their church family. We, as members of the body of Christ, need to be aware of the situations others may be going through, and must be understanding and encouraging because some of us are hurting greatly.

On March 11, 2011, there was a tsunami in northern Japan. The total damages amounted to $300 billion. The death toll reached 15,891. Families were torn apart, homes were swept away, and the world that so many had once known was now gone. Imagine your hometown being swept away in a matter of minutes. It was a dark day for the nation of Japan.

One little town named Otsuchi, established 100 years prior, had grown into a thriving, bustling community. However, in 30 minutes it was gone—almost totally flattened by the tsunami. Out of the nearly 16,000 who died in Japan, 2,500 are still missing. Of those missing persons, 421 lived in the town of Otsuchi. Scars from the devastation remain today.

The radio program, *This American Life*, aired an episode called "One Last Thing Before I Go." They discussed how the people of Otsuchi have coped with their loss of loved ones. It begins by talking about a man named Itaru Sasaki who was already dealing with the pain of losing his cousin when the tsunami hit. Sasaki had bought an old phone booth, similar to those you might find in London, and placed it in his backyard, complete with an old rotary-style telephone! He didn't connect the phone to the phone grid, because when he was using the booth, he wasn't talking to anyone on this earth: he was talking to his deceased cousin. Thus, he called the booth "The Wind Phone."

It was after the tsunami hit that the news spread of The Wind Phone. People began streaming in from all over Japan to use this booth to communicate with their deceased loved ones. The local TV station received permission to record some of the calls in the booth, and the audio recordings are heartbreaking. In one, an elderly lady walks into the booth, picks up the telephone, and dials the number to her house that used to be in Otsuchi. She never says anything, but you can tell she is waiting, hoping that her loved one might answer the call. When no one answers she hangs up the phone, breaks down, and cries.

In another recording there was a man whose wife went missing. He enters the phone booth on a cold winter morning, picks up the phone, begins sobbing, and then begs and pleads for her to return home. He promises her that he will build her a new house if she would just come home to him. "Where are you?" he asks. "Please come home," he says.

Application

Here we are several years after the 2011 tsunami, and it's plain to see that there are many people who are still hurting. The question we ask ourselves is: what are we to do about it?

As members of the body, we must remember that there are large numbers of hurting people and we must be encouraging them to remain involved in the church. Involvement is an excellent way to shift a focus away from sadness, grief, and loss. In order to encourage them, a commitment is required on our part. We must make an effort to include those who are hurting, to surround them with the love and support they are longing for.

I know of a man who lost his wife several years ago, and he made the comment that a few months after becoming a widower, people began to forget that he was still struggling with loss. People began to assume that he was okay, and that he just wanted to be alone. The married couples that he and his wife would go out to dinner with no longer thought of him as part of the group. Members quit asking him to bring food for events, they quit asking him to lead in worship, and they left him out of activities he used to play a big part in. In fairness, he admits that he didn't feel like being around people after losing his wife, but even now he wishes that the members of the church would have included him instead of leaving him alone.

It is stories like this that should motivate us. Instead of assuming, we must put ourselves in the shoes of those who are hurting. We must look to Matthew 7:12 and ask ourselves, "How would I want to be treated if I were in this situation? Would I want people to ignore me, forget about me, and leave me out? No, I would want to be surrounded by those who love me and support me."

Making a commitment to involve those who are hurting is a wonderful thing, but if we ourselves are not involved, how can we expect to help others be involved? A man once asked me, "Do I have to go to church? Can't I just worship from home?" I smiled, thought about his question for a moment, and said, "Being a part of the body of Christ is like being married. How are you going to get to know your spouse if you are never around?" While this may seem like a

Church Involvement

funny analogy, this helps to explain why being involved in the church is of great importance. Who will be there for you when you struggle, or when you are weak? Who will be there to pray for you and support you if you are never around?

How will you become acquainted with other members, how will you grow in the body of Christ if you feel that involvement is not necessary? If we want to help involve others in the body of Christ, we must first make sure we are involved! Involvement can be as simple as bringing food for a potluck, or volunteering to teach a class. The number of things we can do to be involved is limitless!

However, the church cannot grow or thrive if our members believe that involvement is not necessary as part of His body. How can we be evangelistic if we have no connection with the church? How can we grow if we deprive ourselves of the nourishment that comes from being involved in our congregations? Being a part of the congregation not only nourishes us, but it strengthens us. We should remember that the Lord knew Jeremiah before he was created (Jer 1:5). God had a postive plan for the Judeans, even though they were in exile (29:11). I point to these verses to remind us that God knows us better than we know ourselves—He knows our potential. He knows that we can do great things for His kingdom, but it starts with being involved in His church.

Matthew 25:14–30 is where we find the parable of

the talents. The master gave each of his servants several talents, and all but one invested his talent and received more in return. One servant decided it would be better to bury his talent in the dirt. Instead of using what he had been given, he squandered it to the benefit of no one, not even himself. Each and every one of us has a talent that we can use for the benefit of ourselves and others. We can invest it in the church by being involved, and we can watch our investment bring great returns both spiritually and physically. But how can we ever hope to use our talents and encourage our hurting brothers and sisters to remain involved in the church if we aren't even involved?

I pray that those of us who are hurting will read this chapter and realize the importance of being involved in our local congregations. From the beginning, God saw that it was not good for man to be alone. Sometimes we face various trials and feel as though the best thing for us to do is to marginalize ourselves from our brothers and sisters. However, this leads to more pain and sorrow. Let's not forget that God has great plans for us, plans for our welfare, to give us a future and hope.

I also pray that we, as members of the church, will make a commitment to (1) be involved in our local congregation so that we might invest our talents and see great rewards. God knows our potential and believes that we can make a difference in this world. Why else would he give us so many opportunities to

Church Involvement

serve others? Also, let's not forget that being a part of the body of Christ is like being married. How are you going to get to know your spouse if you are never around? (2) Make a goal to generate a renewed effort to include those who might be marginalized and encourage those who are hurting to remain connected to the church. Without the support of its members, the church will never blossom into a thriving community of interdependent members all striving to live and grow in Christ.

Discussion

1. Why do you think hurting people often feel marginalized within the church?
2. List some activities that you could include hurting members in.
3. Why do some members feel that it is not necessary to be involved in the church?
4. List some church-related activities that you could invest in.

13. HAVING REALISTIC EXPECTATIONS
TRAVIS HARMON

Matthew 11:1–15

One Main Thing

"Expectation is the root of all heartache." (Attributed to Shakespeare). We need to have realistic expectations of what our life will be like as a Christian. People who expect one thing and receive something different often become disillusioned and give up. Giving up is something a Christian must never do.

Introduction

One major goal of premarital counseling is to get the couple to have realistic expectations of what their lifelong commitment will look like. If you expect marriage to be a 24 hour per day/seven day per week thrill ride of love and blissful wonderfulness, you may end up

Having Realistic Expectations

being very surprised. Marriage is actually a lot like real life. In fact, it is exactly like real life. When some of that real life sets in on a newlywed couple that expected a "happily ever after" fairy tale, something bad is the inevitable result. Divorce is often the tragic end of that scenario, and the cause is unrealistic expectations that were held at the beginning.

Many Christians fall away because Christianity does not turn out to be what they thought when they originally made their lifelong commitment. When you became "clothed in Christ," you may have thought, "Okay, everything is going to be better from here on out!" If you did, you are not alone. Most new Christians feel that way. Christianity, however, is a lot like real life, and when real life sets in, we have to be ready to stand by Christ in the good times and the bad.

It is easy to have false expectations of what Jesus will do for us. There is an episode in the life of John the Baptist where he appears to struggle with his expectations of Jesus. In Matthew 3:1–10, John is preaching that justice is about to be served and the "coming wrath" will soon break on the enemies of God. John expected Jesus to be the deliverer of Israel and he is very excited to see it happen. However, a little later as John is wasting away in prison (Matt 11:2), this "Messiah" is preaching around the countryside, healing people, and taking boat rides. John begins to question his assumptions. He starts to wonder if this is the Messiah after all and then sends messengers to Jesus asking, "Are You the Coming One, or do we look for another?" (Matt 11:3).

The obvious question that seems to follow is, "If you are the 'Coming One,' then why am I about to die here in this prison?"

Interpretation

John probably asked, "Are you the one we were expecting?" Jesus had failed to meet their expectations. John, like every Jew, was looking for a "Messiah" who as king and military leader would crush the Romans and drive them out of Israel, restoring Israel to the great nation it was long ago. John must have thought Jesus was going to restore Israel to its former glory and that he (John) would be restored also. When that failed to happen, doubt crept in. John knows that Jesus is the Messiah in Matt 3. However, by chapter 11 John is having serious doubts spring up because his circumstances did not meet his expectations. It is easy to see why John begins to wonder if Jesus was "The Coming One" as he waits to die in his Roman prison cell. What John expects does not match his reality.

Application

It sounds incredibly harsh, but we have high expectations of Jesus and of what Christianity will do for us. Sometimes those expectations are disappointed. Our

Having Realistic Expectations

expectations are usually disappointed because of the circumstances in which we find ourselves. In a small place in our hearts (and sometimes in a large place), we expect that if we believe and live right, we will have great marriages, healthy bank balances, well-behaved children, and freedom from major health problems. That is not *really* the way it works. Life will still happen after you give your life to God. People will still hurt you. You will still get sick. You will still lose loved ones in tragic accidents that you will never be able to understand. That does not make God unreal, and it does not mean you should stop being a Christian. It means you are living in the real world. If you are disappointed in or mad at God, it may mean your expectations of Christianity were wrong. Matthew 6:30 is not saying you will never be hungry. You may starve to death as a Christian. Matthew 6:33 is saying seek the Kingdom first anyway, and He will take care of you. It just may not be in the way you expect.

You may live a life of ease, and everything may be wonderful everyday of your life after you become a Christian. Or you may suffer. It may be hard to be a Christian some days. You may be tortured like many were in the first century. Peter was beaten and jailed (Acts 5:41). We do not often suffer now as Christians, but that does not mean we will not or that we cannot. We may be called to suffer from time to time. We may be called to endure hardship with an unwavering faith like Job in the Bible (Jas 5:11).

In a lot of ways, Christianity calls you to do hard things:

- Study God's Word
- Be involved in evangelism
- Become a part of a church, attend, and take part in worship
- Love people, even the ones that are hard to love
- Avoid sin and do not do the things you did before you became a Christian
- Do not retaliate when you are insulted
- Forgive

Conclusion

God never promised to give us our reward in this life. He does promise to reward us in the next life. We want both and expect both, but that is not the arranged deal.

Heaven is a place of rest. This is a place of work, and work is not always easy. Revelation 22:12 says, "And, behold, I come quickly; and my reward is with me, to give every man according as his work shall be." God has expectations for us also. He expects us to trust Him and to obey Him in this life. If we do, He has a reward waiting for us that is beyond our comprehension. God calls us to a life of challenge, not a life of ease.

Do not expect to become a Christian and have

everything magically become easier. It may, but it may also get much, much harder. Life did get harder for the early Christians.

Have realistic expectations of Christianity so that you never quit and that you receive the actual reward that is promised to you (Gal 6:5). Starting with Eve, it has always been the devil's game to create false expectations. We will receive the reward if we do not give up. In times of great disappointment or pain, we should turn toward our God, not away.

Rodney Dangerfield once joked that he and his wife were happy for 20 years, and then they met. Despite all the jokes and cynicism, marriage is a truly beautiful and rewarding life. If both partners are committed to each other and faithful to their vows, there are rewards to being married that are inexpressibly wonderful! There will still be good times and bad. Comparably, when you are baptized, you make a life-long vow of faithfulness much like putting on a wedding ring. You may not live happily ever after but the reward of being a Christian is that you will live happily in the "hereafter" (Rev 21:4).

Discussion

1. Does the Bible teach that we will never suffer as a Christian? Why do we get mad at

God when we do suffer (Rom 5:3; Jas 1:2; 1 Pet 3:14)?
2. What does Paul mean in Romans 8:18?
3. In Genesis 3, how does the serpent play with Eve's expectations? What emotions do you think lead Adam and Eve to hide? Compare what we should do with what we often do after we sin (1 John 1:9; Acts 8:24; John 7:38–50; 8:8–11).
4. How have your expectations of what Christianity was going to be like been different than your reality? Have your expectations of other Christians ever been disappointed?
5. When we get married, we get a license, have a ceremony, exchange vows and sometimes rings. When we commit our life to Christ, what do we do (Acts 2:38; 8:29–39; Gal 3:27)?
6. Have people's expectations of Jesus's return been disappointed (2 Pet 3:3–7)?

BIBLIOGRAPHY

Garland, David E. *2 Corinthians*. New American Commentary 29. Nashville, TN: Broadman and Holman, 1999.

Goetzmann, J. "Conversion." *New International Dictionary of New Testament Theology*. Edited by Colin Brown. 4 vols. Grand Rapids, MI: Zondervan, 1975–1978.

Hawkins, Greg L. and Cally Parkinson. *Move: What 1,000 Churches Reveal About Spiritual Growth*. Grand Rapids, MI: Zondervan, 2011.

Louw, Johannes P., and Eugene A. Nida. *Greek-English Lexicon of the New Testament: Based on Semantic Domains*. 2 vols. New York: American Bible Society, 1989.

Bibliography

Roper, David. *Acts 1–14*. Truth for Today Commentary. Searcy, AR: Resource Publications, 2002.

Smietana, Bob. LifeWayResearch.com: 2014.

Warden, Duane Warden *1&2 Peter and Jude*. Truth for Today Commentary. Searcy, AR: Resource Publications, 2009.

Scripture Index

Old Testament
Genesis

1–2	35
1:1	21
1:27	36
3	43, 100
3:15	43
12	23
18:2	41

Exodus

15:17	43
20:2	18
25:22	43
29:44–46	43

Leviticus

23	43

Deuteronomy

1:39	18
4:9–10	18
4:25	18
5:6	18
6:20–24	17
6:20–25	17
11:1–19	18
26:1–11	17
32:46	18

Joshua

24:2–28	17

1 Samuel

1	13

Nehemiah

9	21, 23
9:6–31	19
9:6–37	16–17, 19
9:31	19
9:32	19
9:32–37	23
9:37	19

Psalms

23	25
25:8	37
51	13
78	17
100:3	25
104	21
105	17–19
105:1–3	18
105:8–11	18
105:24	18
105:37	18
105:39	18
105:45	18
106	17–19
106:1–2	18
106:6–7	18
106:8	19
106:10	19
106:13	18
106:19–21	18
106:24	18
106:43–44	19
106:47–48	18
135	17
136	17, 37
145:13	37

Isaiah

45:25	47
59:1–2	43

Scripture Index

62:5	35	22:37	3–4
Jeremiah		23:27	2
1:5	91	24:51	75
29:11	91	25:14–30	86, 91
New Testament		27:5	79
Matthew		28	58
1:1–17	21	28:18	75
3	96	28:18–20	57, 59, 62
3:1–10	95	28:19	69, 80
3:15	80	28:20	37
4:10	42	**Mark**	
4:18–22	65	1:1–3	21
5:1–16	65	1:4–5	80
5:3–12	2	1:35	10
5:8	2	6:46	9
5:9	36	9:28–29	10
5:13–15	39	**Luke**	
5:16	39	1:1	21
6:7	11	2:37	8, 13
6:7–15	11	3:21–22	9
6:30	97	4	8
6:33	97	4:14	9
7:12	37, 90	5:16	10
7:13–14	39	6:12	9, 11
9:9–13	66	6:40	64
10:5–15	66	9:10–17	10
11	96	9:18–20	9
11:1–15	94	9:28	9
11:2	95	9:37–42	10
11:3	95	11	12
11:18–20	38	11:1	8–10, 13
12:49–50	63	11:5	12
15:6–9	72	11:10	12
16:1–18	9	11:13	12
17:1–8	72	14	53
18:15	32	18:1	10

Scripture Index

18:9–14	3	2:46	42
18:13	3	2:47	80
22:39–46	9	3:14	20
22:54–62	79	3:17–21	78
23:34	10	5:41	97
23:46	10	6:10–11	19
23:47	20	7	19, 21
24:30–35	22	7:2–53	17

John

1:1–5	21	7:51–53	19
2:20	44	7:52	20
3:16	1, 35	8:12	81
3:22	80	8:24	100
3:26	80	8:29–39	100
4:21–24	42	8:38	81
5:25–30	72	10:47	81
5:26–27	71	13:16–41	17
7:38–50	100	16:14–15	81
8:8–11	100	17:30–31	78
10:11	25–26	19:4	80
13:34–35	35	20:7	42
14:6	38	20:21	78
15:1–8	38	22:16	81
15:11	35	24:15	38
17	9	26:20	78
21:15–21	79		

Romans

Acts

1:1	21	1:2	21
2	78	1:16	58
2:36	78	2:3–4	37
2:37	78	2:4	36
2:37–39	37	3:3	37
2:38	77, 80–81, 100	3:23	77
		3:24–25	83
2:42	42	5:3	100
2:42–47	77	5:8	35
		6:1–7	81
		6:11	77, 82, 84

Scripture Index

6:12	82	**2 Corinthians**	
6:12–23	82	5:17	49–50
6:13	82	7:9–10	79
6:17–18	81–82	7:10	79
6:19	82	10:1	37
6:20–23	38	12:20	31
6:22	82	**Galatians**	
8:18	100	1:1–5	21
8:26–28	13	2:20	82
11:22	37	3:26–27	44, 75
12:1–2	4	3:27	50, 81, 100
12:3–8	5	5:19–21	34, 39
12:4–5	87	5:22–23	34
12:9–21	6	5:22–25	5
12:10	37	6:5	99
12:16	38	**Ephesians**	
14:11	47	1:11–12	38
15:13	35	1:22–23	75
15:14	37	2:4–7	36
15:33	36	4:11–16	14
16:20	36	4:17–24	81
1 Corinthians		6:10	82
1:10	36	**Philippians**	
1:11	14	1:2	35
4:14–17	37	1:6	22
7:5	38	1:7	35
7:9	38	2:2	5
11:18	42	2:3	4–5
11:20–29	43	2:5	38
11:26	21	2:10	47
12:13	81	2:15	39
13:1–8	6	3:17	14
13:1–13	35	4:4	35
14:26–40	42	4:5–7	38
14:33	36	4:6–7	4
15:23–28	72	4:7	6

Scripture Index

4:9	6	5:12	50–51
Colossians		5:14	51
1:3	13	6:1	55
1:9–12	36	7:27	44
1:10–18	72	10:1–22	44
2:11–12	81	10:19–22	45
3:12–15	6	10:22–31	40, 42
3:12–17	37	11	17
3:17	75	11:6	45
3:24	75	13:5	37
4:12	13	13:17	28–29
1 Thessalonians		**James**	
1:2	13	1:1	21
2:13	13	1:2	100
5:12–13	30	1:2–4	36
5:23–24	36	1:13	38
2 Thessalonians		1:17	37
1:11–12	37	4:8	45
1 Timothy		5:11	97
1:11	35	5:16	54
1:17	36	**1 Peter**	
2:1–7	13	1:1	21
3	29	1:20	21
2 Timothy		2:2	50
2:2	37	3:14	100
2:15	4	3:21	81
2:22	36	5	27
3:16	13	5:1–3	30
3:16–17	4	5:2	26
Titus		5:5	25, 27–28
1	29	**2 Peter**	
2:1–6	38	3:3–7	100
3:4–5	37	3:18	1, 50
Hebrews		**1 John**	
1:1–2	72	1	83
2:1–3	46	1:5	83

Scripture Index

1:6	83
1:7a	83
1:7b	83
1:9	83, 100
2:1–2	13
3:16	35
4:8	35
4:16	35
4:19	20

Revelation

1:8	21
21:3–4	22
21:4	99
22:12	98
22:13	21
22:20	21–22

CREDITS

Select Scripture quotations are taken from the NEW AMERICAN STANDARD BIBLE®, copyright© 1960, 1962, 1963, 1968, 1971, 1972, 1973, 1975, 1977, 1995 by The Lockman Foundation. Used by permission.

Select Scripture quotations are taken from the NEW KING JAMES VERSION®. Copyright© 1982 by Thomas Nelson, Inc. Used by permission. All rights reserved.

Select Scripture quotations are taken from the NEW REVISED STANDARD VERSION BIBLE, copyright © 1989 National Council of the Churches of Christ in the United States of America. Used by permission. All rights reserved worldwide.

Select Scriptures quotations are taken from the Holy Bible, New International Version®, NIV®. Copyright © 1973, 1978, 1984, 2011 by Biblica, Inc.™ Used by permission of Zondervan. All rights reserved worldwide. www.zondervan.com The "NIV" and "New International Version" are trademarks registered in the United States Patent and Trademark Office by Biblica, Inc.®

Scripture quotations marked HCSB are been taken from the Holman Christian Standard Bible®, Copyright © 1999, 2000, 2002, 2003 by Holman Bible Publishers. Used by permission. Holman Christian Standard Bible®, Holman CSB®, and HCSB® are federally registered trademarks of Holman Bible Publishers.

Scripture quotations from The Authorized (King James) Version. Rights in the Authorized Version in the United Kingdom are vested in the Crown. Reproduced by permission of the Crown's patentee, Cambridge University Press.

Scripture quotations are from the ESV® Bible (The Holy Bible, English Standard Version®), copyright © 2001 by Crossway, a publishing ministry of Good News Publishers. Used by permission. All rights reserved

CONTRIBUTORS

Bill Bagents (DMin Amridge University) is Professor of Ministry, Counseling and Biblical Studies at Heritage Christian University.

Jeremy Barrier (PhD Brite Divinity School, Texas Christian University) is Professor of Biblical Literature at Heritage Christian University.

Jim Collins (MMin Amridge University) retired as the Director of Enrollment at Heritage Christian University.

Nathan Daily (PhD Claremont Graduate University) is Heritage Christian University Registrar and Assistant Professor of Religion.

Arvy Dupuy (MA Amridge University) is Adjunct Instructor at HCU.

Philip Goad (MMin in progress Heritage Christian University) preaches for North Highlands

Church of Christ in Russellville, Alabama and serves as Director of Alumni Relations at Heritage Christian University.

Justin Guin (MDiv Freed-Hardeman University) is Adjunct Instructor at Heritage Christian University as serves as Youth Minister with the Double Springs Church of Christ in Double Springs, Alabama.

Travis Harmon (MMin Heritage Christian University) is Vice President of Student Services and Instructor of Ministry at HCU.

Matt Heupel (MMin Freed-Hardeman University) is Adjunct Instructor at Heritage Christian University and preaches for the Woodlawn Church of Christ in Florence, Alabama.

C. Wayne Kilpatrick (MAR Harding School of Theology) is Emeritus Professor of Church History at Heritage Christian University.

Brad McKinnon (PhD in progress Aberdeen Univer-sity) is Associate Professor and Director of Field Education at Heritage Christian University

Ray Reynolds (MMin Heritage Christian University) is Director of T.I.T.U.S. Camp held on the campus of Heritage Christian University.

Lucas Suddreth (MDiv in progress Harding School of Theology) serves as Young Adult Minister at Germantown Church of Christ in Germantown, Tennessee.

BEREAN STUDY SERIES

The Ekklesia of Christ (2015)

What Real Christianity Looks Like (2016)

Clothed in Christ (2017)

Instructions of Living (2018)

Visions of Grace (2019)

Cloud of Witnesses (2020)

For the Glory of God (2021)

Majesty and Mercy (2022)

To see full catalog of Heritage Christian University Press and its imprint Cypress Publications, visit www.hcu.edu/publications.

www.ingramcontent.com/pod-product-compliance
Lightning Source LLC
Chambersburg PA
CBHW070919080526
44589CB00013B/1361